# THINKING WITH
# CONCEPTS

# THINKING WITH CONCEPTS

BY

JOHN WILSON

CAMBRIDGE UNIVERSITY PRESS

CAMBRIDGE

LONDON   NEW YORK   NEW ROCHELLE

MELBOURNE   SYDNEY

WILSON

Published by the Press Syndicate of the University of Cambridge
The Pitt Building, Trumpington Street, Cambridge CB2 1RP
32 East 57th Street, New York, NY 10022, USA
10 Stamford Road, Oakleigh, Melbourne 3166, Australia

© Cambridge University Press 1963

First published 1963
Reprinted 1966, 1969, 1971, 1972, 1974,
1976, 1978, 1979, 1980, 1982, 1983, 1985

Printed in the United States of America

ISBN 0 521 06825 8 hard covers
ISBN 0 521 09601 4 paperback

# CONTENTS

# PREFACE

This is not a book about 'straight thinking' or 'clear thinking'. I know that there are books about this sort of thing, some of them very useful (like Susan Stebbing's *Thinking to Some Purpose*). They help the reader to become aware of his own prejudice and irrationality by discussing and illustrating the dangers of bias, fallacies, irrelevancy, not checking the facts, and so on. But their use is limited, since the methods used to teach so wide and ill-defined a subject as 'straight thinking' are bound to be eclectic and heterogeneous: they leave the reader more aware of the importance of reason and language, certainly: but they do not equip him with a single, coherent technique of thought which he can apply for himself over a wide field.

But such a technique exists. It was established about thirty years ago, and though it has suffered from being tied too tightly to the apron-strings of certain schools of modern philosophy, it has made a good deal of headway since then: indeed it would be reasonable to say that, in a quiet way, it has caused something like a revolution in our approach to questions of a certain type.

I have called this technique 'the analysis of concepts' because it is designed to handle and clarify concepts in a particular way. It provides one with a specialised and appropriate method which one can be taught to use in answering many of the more important and interesting questions which can be asked. Conceptual understanding is also required, of course, in many other contexts. Most subjects at sixth-form level necessitate the understanding of concepts peculiar to those subjects, and it is a mistake to suppose that such understanding seeps automatically into the pupil's mind. The use of conceptual analysis for education in the broader sense is also obvious, nor shall I here argue its value for adults in terms of improved communication and understanding. The importance of the aims of conceptual analysis is generally agreed. What is not fully grasped is that conceptual analysis is a specialised subject in its own right, with its own techniques: that general questions, and indeed all questions involving abstract concepts, cannot be tackled without these techniques in any but the most feeble and confused manner: and that the techniques can in fact be taught and learned quite easily.

This is not, then, primarily a book to be read in one's spare time, for the sake of what my sixth formers at least have the ghastly habit of calling 'general culture'. It is a book to be worked through: in a sense, a text-book. I have myself taught these techniques, not without success and certainly without undue difficulty and boredom, to sixth forms for some years: certainly they have produced better results than the rather vague 'general periods' which one might otherwise have given, and which often seem too purposeless and unmethodical both to boys and masters who are concerned with specialised studies in an acutely competitive environment. Moreover, to be quite honest, I feel that a great many adults who are concerned with matters of general interest and importance—religion, politics, morality, social studies, science, or even just personal relationships—would do better to spend less time in simply accepting the concepts of others uncritically, and more

time in learning how to analyse concepts in general.
Conceptual analysis gives framework and purposiveness
to thinking that might otherwise meander indefinitely
and purposelessly among the vast marshes of intellect
and culture.

The book is divided into four parts. In chapter I
I shall try to explain what the relevant techniques are
and how they can be deployed effectively. It is important to master this chapter thoroughly before moving
on. In chapters II and IV respectively I apply these
techniques to particular concepts, and give the reader
some examples on which to practise. The application of
the techniques in these two chapters is made in two
contexts:

(i) conceptual criticism of passages written by
other people;

(ii) the answering of conceptual questions.

Chapter III includes some general remarks on philosophy and analysis, for the benefit of those who wish to
proceed further with the subject. These are arranged
in this order because it is an order which, for most
people, moves from what is more easy to what is
more difficult. It is easiest to start with a passage
written by someone else, because the passage itself helps
one to start thinking: there is something to get one's
teeth into, and so one does not feel completely lost. It is
not too hard to move from this to the context of a particular question: the existence of a question (like the
existence of the passage, though to a lesser extent) gives
some sort of shape to one's thinking. From this we can
move to the more difficult business of thinking about
concepts in the abstract. Here one has to think of the
ways in which the concept is used without the help

either of someone else's writing or of a particular question.

In a sense the book is specifically designed to meet the needs of those many sixth formers who have to face the all-important General Paper for entrance to the university, and particularly those who enter for a university place or an award in 'general studies' or 'social studies', where the bulk of the papers are general papers of a logical or conceptual nature. In all these papers questions involving the analysis of concepts are invariably (and rightly) set, and many of them demand conceptual criticism of given passages also. But such an approach is equally suitable also for the ordinary adult who wishes to master these techniques, or indeed for the pupil who is studying them even though he is not threatened with an examination. For this is a serious subject, and it must be tackled methodically.

### ACKNOWLEDGEMENTS

I should like to express my thanks to those many people who have helped me by criticism and conversation: in particular to Mr and Mrs C. H. Rieu.

### NOTE

It has not been easy to find suitable passages for comment in chapter II. In order to simplify the issues for students who will tackle these passages, I have in some cases omitted some words and phrases which appeared in the authors' original writing: though I have added nothing of my own. I have attempted to ensure that this has not involved any real misrepresentation or distortion of the original arguments.

J. B. W.

CHAPTER I

# THE BUSINESS OF ANALYSIS

## I. WHAT IS CONCEPTUAL ANALYSIS?

This book is designed to give the reader mastery over certain skills and techniques. Half the battle is won if you can get a clear idea of exactly what these skills and techniques are, and what purpose they serve: so we shall have to begin by spending a lot of time over this point. Techniques like being able to solve quadratic equations, doing Latin prose, or translating German into English are difficult to master: but at least we have the advantage of knowing just what it is that we are supposed to be doing, even if we do not always do it very well. These techniques and many others have for a long time been placed under different headings: they are what schools call 'subjects'—mathematics, Latin, German, and so on. Often we can look up the right answers to questions in these subjects, by referring to a dictionary, or a grammar, or an authoritative textbook. But none of this applies to the techniques outlined in this book. That is partly because they are new techniques: we have only become fully conscious of them in the last twenty or thirty years. But it is chiefly because of the nature of the techniques themselves, and the general purpose which they serve.

What are these techniques *like*? They are not like 'subjects' such as Latin or mathematics, which have clear-cut and well-defined rules, and in which answers are indisputably right or wrong. They are rather more like specific skills such as the ability to swim well or play a good game of football. But they are most of all like general skills which have wide application, such as the skills we refer to when we talk of 'seamanship', or 'having a good eye', or 'being able to express oneself'. These general skills are useful in a great many different activities; thus seamanship is useful in sailing, manning a lifeboat, rescuing people from a wreck, and so on: having a good eye is a great advantage in any ball game: and the ability to express oneself in words helps us in writing essays, letters and reports, as well as in making our feelings and needs clear to other people. Yet though the skills come into many different activities, we can see that the same skills are at work in each case. To take one more example: although we spend a lot of time mixing with other people in many different circumstances—at home, at school, in the army, in a factory, on holiday—yet we can still distinguish a special skill or ability which we call 'being able to get on well with other people'. This skill is something which we can cultivate: but we can see that learning such a skill is going to be very different from learning Latin or mathematics.

We can most easily grasp the nature of these techniques by looking at the sort of questions which they help us to answer. Consider first a pair of questions:

   (i) Is a whale able to sink a 15,000 ton liner?

   (ii) Is a whale a fish?

We can describe the first as a question of fact. To be in a position to answer it, all we have to do is to find out the relevant facts: either by personal experience, or by getting reliable information from others. We may have to put the facts together and work the problem out: thus we may be able to answer the question without actually having seen a whale sink a ship, and without having been reliably told that it can—if, for instance, we knew the weight and speed of whales, the thickness of ships' hulls, and so on. But even in this case we would not be straying beyond the realm of fact. To answer the question, we need only knowledge about the world and some things in the world. But the second question is not like this. We might know all the relevant facts about whales and about fish, and still be in doubt about how to answer it. For instance, we might know that whales suckle their young like other mammals, and that they swim like other fish, and a great many other facts about them. But this might still leave us undecided, because we would not be sure whether a creature of this kind counts as a fish or not. We would still have to ask a question like 'Does a whale (being what it is) come into the category of "fish", or not?'

It is important to notice that this is not a question like the question about the whale and the liner. It is a question of a certain distinct kind, a kind which the techniques we have mentioned are designed to deal with. I shall call these questions by the general name of *questions of concept*. Thus, in this example, the word 'fish' does not just stand for lots of actual fish swimming around in the sea: it also represents an idea, a concept of what a 'fish' is—what the word designates in our language. We can see this best by repeating this particular question in various forms. Thus we could ask 'Does a whale come under the concept of fish, as we

normally use that concept?' or 'Does the concept of
fish normally include things like whales?' or 'Does
what we normally mean by "a fish" cover whales or
not?' To rephrase the question in these ways, which
may seem unnecessary and fussy, draws attention to the
point that the question is about *meaning*: what we want
to know is what we normally mean by 'fish', how one
verifies whether something is a fish or not, what *counts*
as a fish.

We can also notice another thing about this question,
which may seem curious. The answer depends on what
is meant by 'fish': and it is a mistake to think that 'fish'
means one thing and one thing only. If you are a pro-
fessional biologist or an expert on fish, you will probably
say that a whale is not a fish, or 'not really' a fish:
because biologists classify creatures in such a way that
mammals come into one group and fish into another.
Creatures which are mammals, like whales, are by this
not allowed to count as fish: the concept of fish excludes
mammals. But if you are working in the Ministry of
Agriculture and Fisheries (which deals with whales
along with everything else that swims in the sea), you
will probably not pay much attention to this biological
classification: you will have a classification of your own,
which will include whales in the concept of fish. The
ordinary person, unless he happens to know some
biology, would probably also call a whale a fish. Thus
whether you call a whale a fish or not depends entirely
on what angle you look at it from. Nor can we say that
one viewpoint is better than another—that the biologist,
for instance, has a better right to an opinion than
the Minister of Agriculture and Fisheries. One view-

point is better for some purposes, another for other purposes.

We can see these points more clearly, and go rather more deeply into them, if we take another pair of examples. Consider the questions:

(i) Is a flying-boat capable of landing on choppy water?

(ii) Is a flying-boat a boat or an aeroplane?

Again we can see that the first is a straightforward question of fact, the second a more complex question of concept. To answer the first we need personal or second-hand experience and observation: to answer the second we need to consider the concepts *boat* and *aeroplane*, and see into which category a flying-boat would come. And again, we can see that there is no single right answer for all circumstances. If one is concerned with, say, mooring-space in a river, or protecting seabirds from being disturbed while nesting, one would count a flying-boat as a boat: whereas if one is concerned with dropping bombs, or swiftness of travel, one would count it as an aeroplane. It is a mistake to say that it is 'really' a boat or 'really' an aeroplane. Once one knows what a flying-boat in fact is—once one has described all its characteristics—it is a matter of the particular circumstances whether one calls it a boat or an aeroplane.

But even though it is a question of *concept* and not of simple *fact*, it makes a big difference how we decide to use our concepts: our decisions can be wise or unwise. For instance, if we asked a clerk at an airline office whether there was an aeroplane which could take us to New York by Tuesday, and he said 'No', we should be justifiably annoyed to find that although there were no ordinary aeroplanes there was in fact a flying-boat. And if we approached the clerk and said 'Look here, you've misled me: there's a flying-boat which leaves at just the time I want. Why didn't you tell me about it?', and the clerk said 'Oh, well, flying-boats aren't aeroplanes, they're boats', we should still be annoyed. We should think that the clerk had been stupid in his application of the concepts of a boat and an aeroplane. The point here is that words are meant to serve human purposes and desires, and must be used in such a way as to serve them efficiently. The clerk was stupid because he did not grasp the general context and purpose of our inquiry, which was concerned only with getting some quick means of transport to New York: in the light of this context and purpose flying-boats ought to count as aeroplanes. The clerk might do well in a harbour-master's office, where they are concerned with buoys and mooring-space and where flying-boats ought to count as boats: but he is no good in an airline.

This is a very simple example which shows the nature of a question of concept in its basic essentials: but it may be inadequate to show that such questions are of great practical importance. Airline clerks are not often as stupid as that. But now suppose we ask another question of concept: 'Is psychology a science?' We would first find out the facts about psychology, and perhaps end up by agreeing that it had some things in common with sciences like physics and chemistry, and some characteristics which were quite different: so that it was a matter of choice whether we called it a science or not. Now the choice might seem purely academic. But suppose we are called on to decide the question before a committee which had the power to give large sums of money for research in science. The committee might say 'Now tell us, is psychology really a science, or is it more like astrology and crystal-gazing and witchcraft?' We might then have to choose whether to put psychology in the 'science' category, or in the 'astrology-and-witchcraft' category: and whichever we did, it would have a very considerable effect on the future of the subject. We might decide to call it a science, or not to call it a science: or we might want to invent a third category, and call it perhaps 'in principle a science' or 'a potential science'. It would be very important to be quite clear about the concepts in this case: we could not begin to make a sensible choice until we had analysed and understood what was meant by 'science' or 'a potential science'. This is obviously more difficult than understanding the concepts of an aeroplane and a boat.

Before moving on to consider the more complex questions of concept with which our techniques deal, however, we must try to state more clearly what exactly it is that we are concerned with when we analyse concepts. We know we are not concerned with finding new facts. It is also important to realise that we are not concerned with values or moral judgements, with what is actually right or wrong, good or bad. Consider these three questions:

(i) Is Communism likely to spread all over the world?

(ii) Is Communism a desirable system of government?

(iii) Is Communism compatible with democracy?

The first question is a question of fact. We may not be able to give a definite answer which we could prove to be right, because the question asks us to predict the future: but the only relevant evidence for our answer consists of facts about Communism and about the world. The answer may be doubtful, but it is not doubtful because we are in doubt about either the *value* of Communism or the *concept* of Communism: it is only doubtful because we are not certain which way the facts point—or perhaps we just need more facts. The second question, on the other hand, asks us to assign some kind of value to Communism: we are asked whether it is good or bad, wise or unwise, right or wrong, politically desirable or undesirable. This, then, is a question of value. But the third question is a question of concept. We have to consider whether the concept of Communism fits or does not fit into the concept of democracy. As usual, the answer may turn out to be a matter of choice in the end: probably it partly fits, and partly fails to fit. There would be no point in asking a question of concept if the answer was obvious: a question like 'Is tyranny compatible with democracy?' is silly, because we all know that the concepts are diametrically opposed.

What are we really dealing with, then, when we analyse concepts, if we are not dealing with facts or values? In a sense it is true that we are 'just dealing with words'—words like 'boat', 'science', 'democracy' and so on. But it is misleading to say this, because it implies that we are dealing with something that has no real or practical importance: whereas we have seen, in the cases of the airline clerk and the committee deciding on research grants for science, that the way in which we decide to fix our concepts (or use our words, if you like) is of considerable importance. One might say, if one was sitting on a jury and asked to decide whether a prisoner was guilty or not guilty, 'Oh, well, it just depends what you mean by "guilty", it's just a matter of words and definitions': and this would be very misleading.

We said earlier that questions of concept were concerned with meaning: and though this too is true, it is inadequate. Suppose that we say that the question 'Is a flying-boat a boat?' is concerned with the meaning of the word 'boat'. It is a little queer to say this, because we know perfectly well what the word 'boat' means. It is not a particularly unusual or extraordinary word, like 'asymptotic' or 'polymorphous': if we know French or German, we can translate it into those languages without difficulty. This is also true of more complex words like 'science', 'Communism', 'democracy' and so on. In one sense we know quite well what these words mean; and if we did not, we could always look them up in a dictionary. To take another example: suppose someone said 'That's a good book', and we asked him 'What do you mean, a *good* book?' This is a perfectly reasonable question: and it is also a question of concept, because what we want to know is what counts as 'a good book' with him. (It is as if someone said 'Communism is perfectly democratic', and we were to ask 'What do you mean, democratic?') Yet it would be wrong to say that we were asking for the meaning of the word 'good'. 'Good' is a very common word, which we use correctly every day: it means, roughly, 'to be commended' or 'to be approved' or 'desirable'. We know this already. Yet we still ask 'What do you mean, a *good* book?'

The best way of looking at this point is to say that in questions of concept we are not concerned with *the* meaning of a word. Words do not have only one meaning: indeed, in a sense they do not have meaning in their own right at all, but only in so far as people use them in different ways. It is better to say that we are concerned with *actual and possible uses* of words. That is why it is no use looking up the word in a dictionary: it will not help. When we ask 'What do you mean, a *good* book?' what we are really saying is 'What counts as a good book with you?' or 'What are your criteria for a good book?' Sometimes we behave as if all we had to do was to find out the 'real' meaning of a word like 'democracy' or 'boat' or 'science', and then the answer to our question would be obvious. But unfortunately it is not so simple as that: and a moment's thought will show us that words like 'democracy' and 'science'— and even words like 'boat'—do not have 'real meanings'. They just have different uses and different applications: and our job is to analyse the concepts and map out these uses and applications.

In the same way we must not make the mistake of thinking that answering questions of concept is a matter of 'defining one's terms', and that we should begin by producing a definition of 'science', 'democracy', etc. For the whole point of asking such questions is that the definition of these words is unclear: or we might rather say that they do not have definitions, but only uses. Of course there are some words which do have precise definitions: in geometry and mechanics, for instance, words like 'triangle', 'straight line', 'point', and 'force', 'mass' and 'work' are precisely defined. If we are asked 'What is work?' in an examination on mechanics, we know that we have to give the textbook definition. But that is because mechanics is a highly evolved and reasonably precise science, and the examination is testing our knowledge of that science, not our ability to analyse concepts. If we were asked 'What is work?' in a general paper for a university examination, however, our approach would be quite different. We should start thinking about the concept of work as it is used in everyday life, not just in the science of mechanics. And in everyday life there is no definition of 'work': we should have to notice various uses of the word, the different meanings it bears in different contexts, and so on. We should have to analyse the concept.

We have spent some time saying what questions of concept are *not* concerned with: and this is important, because there is a perennial temptation to try and treat such questions as questions of some other kind—partly because the notion of 'questions of concept' and the techniques for dealing with them are both rather new, and partly because it needs a lot of practice to gain a firm grasp of the nature of such questions. Questions of concept, then, are not questions of fact: nor are they questions of value: nor are they questions concerned with *the* meanings of words, or *the* definitions of words. What are they? All we have said so far is that they are concerned with the uses of words, and with the criteria or principles by which those uses are determined. But all this sounds rather vague and we

must try to do better. Let us take another group of
questions:

(i)   Are you free to vote as you wish in Russia?

(ii)  Is freedom to vote as one wishes a good thing?

(iii) Are any of our actions ever really free?

And another group as well:

(i)   Did the Greeks think it right to keep women in
an inferior position to men?

(ii)  Do you think it right to keep women in an
inferior position to men?

(iii) Can one ever be certain about what is right?

We know enough now to identify the first question in
both groups as a question of fact, the second as a question of value, and the third as a question of concept.
Yet the same words appear throughout each group:
'free' is used throughout the first group, and 'right'
throughout the second. But in the first and second
questions in each group it is assumed that we know
quite well what is meant by 'free' and 'right'—as,
indeed, in a sense we do know. No *logical* problem, no
problem of *meaning or use*, is supposed to arise in questions (i) and (ii). In the third question, however, such
problems do arise.

Observe that, if we were not on the watch for them,
we might easily fail to notice that these were logical
problems. There is nothing in the *form* of the question
which tells us that it is a question of concept. The
grammatical form of 'Are any of our actions ever really
free?' looks like the form of 'Are any of our actions
ever really capable of blowing up the world?', which
would be a question of fact involving knowledge about
nuclear fission, atom bombs, etc. Similarly 'Can one

ever be certain about what is right?' looks like 'Can one ever be certain about tomorrow's weather?', which is a question about meteorology and not about concepts. We have to notice that the appearance of the question is deceptive: and this means that we have to be aware that whereas 'blowing up the world' and 'tomorrow's weather' are not logically mysterious or difficult notions, 'free' and 'right' are logically mysterious.

When we face such questions, we begin to get a sense of this logical mystery. Here are a few more: 'How do we know that all our experience isn't just a dream or an hallucination?', 'Are all men equal?', 'Are all our actions predetermined?', 'What is truth?', 'Is there such a thing as beauty?', 'Are faith and reason opposed to each other?', 'Is there a God?'. It is curious that all these questions contain words with which we are very familiar: words like 'dream', 'equal', 'truth', 'beauty', 'faith', 'reason' and 'God'. Some may include words which look rather more like philosopher's jargon, such as 'predetermined': but in general they use words which are in common use in everyday speech. And yet, somehow, the questions strike us as *queer*. They are not the sort of questions we normally ask in everyday life: or at least, only when we are in the sort of mood to talk about what we commonly call 'abstract' subjects. People do not very often ask themselves, for instance, 'Do I ever really act freely—aren't I under some sort of compulsion all the time?', or say 'Perhaps the whole of life is just a dream'. It is true that questions like 'Is there a God?' are commonly asked, and do not seem particularly queer. But we can come to see that this question is significantly different from questions that might look the same, such as 'Is there life on other planets?' or 'Do unicorns exist?', which are questions of fact. The concept of God is a mysterious concept, even though the word 'God' is one which we may use every day.

Faced with these questions, we are asked to take seriously concepts which hitherto we had taken for granted. We are asked, as it were, to become *self-conscious* about words which hitherto we had used without thinking—not necessarily used wrongly, but used unselfconsciously. This is rather like the process of psychoanalysis, or the self-examinations and confessions practised in religion. In these we are asked to become more conscious of our actions, to look at them objectively and think about them: hitherto we had been content to act, but now we have to become aware of the significance of our actions. In the same way, when we deal with questions of concept, we are asked to become aware of the significance of our words. Once we start this process, we very soon begin to feel baffled. Someone might ask us, perhaps, 'What is time?': and since 'time' is a word we use every day, we might start off gaily by saying 'Time? Well, time is what goes on when one thing happens after another, we use clocks or the sun to tell the time, we talk of the passage of time, it's like a river . . . '; but it soon becomes clear to us that we are unable to give a clear account of the concept.

Questions of concept seem queer, because it is not clear how we should set about answering such questions. 'Are all men equal?' How *could* one answer this? How does one start? What would count as a proper answer? The whole thing is mysterious. 'Equal? What do you mean, equal? Equal to what? Equal in what? What would be the point of saying that all men were equal, or that they weren't? Under what circumstances would one want to say either of these? What practical consequences, would follow if one did? We know what is meant by saying that a line *AB* is equal to a line *CD* in geometry, or that two teams have equal numbers of people; but as for all men being equal, what are we to make of that?' We get the impression of a tangled ball of string which has to be carefully unwound, of a great pile of different objects which have to be sorted, or of a large area of country which we have to map.

Perhaps this last simile can help us a bit further. Making a map of a piece of country, like learning to deal with concepts, is essentially a process of becoming more self-conscious in relation to one's normal environment. We may well have *used* the country for some time, in the sense that we have passed through it, and got to know our way around in it. But we have not become objectively conscious of it in the way that one needs to if one is going to make a map of it. We can find our way from one town to another, and we may know that some parts of the country are hilly, others wooded, and so on; but we cannot sketch it out on paper with any accuracy, because we do not know the country *in that particular way*. Similarly we have all our lives worked with words, used words successfully to communicate with our fellows; but we have not become conscious of the meanings of words.

The process of becoming conscious is not a simple one: not so simple, for instance, as learning a factual subject like physics, or a subject governed by strict rules like mathematics. It is rather like learning to play a game. To play any game well you have to have a clear grasp of what the game is about—what the objective of the game is, what counts as winning—and also plenty of practice. But it is also helpful to listen to advice: for there are quite a few useful principles and precepts. They will not be useful, however, unless taken in the spirit in which they are given. For instance, it is a useful piece of advice in tennis to say 'Keep the arm fully extended, and don't bend the elbow too much'. But there are plenty of occasions—when you are up at the net, for example—when this advice should be disregarded: and it is impossible for the coach to make a complete list of these exceptions, because so much depends on the individual player, on his opponent, on the conditions of the court, and so on. The person being coached must certainly not disregard this advice: but neither must he take it too seriously, or think that if he always follows it he will necessarily play good tennis. He must learn to take the advice in conjunction with practice in playing the game itself, and constantly move back and forth from the advice to the actual situations he meets on the court. Only by so doing will he get the most out of the practice or the advice.

## 2. DIFFICULTIES AND METHODS OF ANALYSIS

### A. *Difficulties of temperament*

At the risk of appearing to be patronising, we must first note some of the psychological obstacles or resistances to the use of our techniques. These obstacles are at once the hardest to overcome and the hardest to describe or explain. It is no part of this book to investigate them in detail: but since they are so important for the practice of the techniques, it may help the reader to have them before him as a reminder—even though they are often obvious and in a sense well known to him.

(1) One of the most worrying things that can afflict people when they start to use these techniques is the feeling of being hopelessly *lost*. Some temperaments, more than others, like everything to be expressed in a neat and tidy way, under separate headings, in the way in which one might take dictated notes when learning history at an elementary level: or perhaps as one might set out an equation in algebra or a theorem in geometry. We have already seen enough to realise that our techniques do not lend themselves to this treatment. Nobody can say: 'There are the following six points about the concept of science: once you have taken these down and memorised them you have learned all there is to learn': or at least if one were to say this, it would be very far from the whole truth. The whole business is far more complex. Often such tidy-minded people feel at the end of a discussion about concepts that no conclusion has been reached: 'they haven't *got* anywhere': nobody has come up with 'the answer'.

(2) In contrast to this, there is also the feeling that questions of concept can be settled much more easily than in fact is the case. People of an intelligent but impatient disposition may feel in the course of discussion that 'the whole thing is a fuss about nothing: obviously such-and-such a concept just means so-and-so: there's no need to go on splitting hairs'. As we shall see, the richness of use and meaning in most interesting concepts

is such that it would be quite possible to discuss the same concept for weeks on end and still have more to learn.

(3) Another contrasting feeling, which sometimes besets those who take easily to the techniques, may be described as a curious compulsion to analyse everything: it is not unlike the desire to interpret everything by psychoanalysis, sometimes felt by those who take easily to psychoanalytic theory or who mix in psychoanalytic circles. Analysis becomes an addiction, so that such people find themselves anxious to analyse not only concepts like science, freedom, democracy and so on, but also perfectly ordinary concepts like table and horse. No doubt there is a sense in which all concepts, even the simplest, are worth analysing: and it must be admitted that some words which seem simple, such as 'all', 'if' or 'is', are among the most important to the student of informal logic. But for practical purposes at least one should be able to single out some concepts for special attention, and leave the rest alone: and for this purpose a sense of proportion is essential.

(4) Next there is the inability or unwillingness to talk or debate, either with oneself or in discussion with others. In most discussions, whether about concepts or other matters, there are usually people who sit silent: who feel, somehow, that there is nothing they can say. It may be that they are frightened of making fools of themselves: but willingness to make a fool of oneself is one of the chief requisites for learning anything—if one does not try (and hence sometimes fail), one can never succeed. This applies also to what we may call internal debate: that is, thinking to oneself, whether silently or aloud. A good deal of constructive thought is like

holding an internal debate or dialectic: you put forward one idea, and then bring up another to challenge it, weigh both ideas against each other, perhaps introduce a third, and so forth. For questions of concept in particular it is very important to say *something*, as it were on trust that it will lead somewhere. It may lead somewhere or it may not: but one cannot even make a beginning unless it is said. Fluency, therefore, in the sense of being able freely and willingly to put forward ideas and statements, is one of the most important things to cultivate: and the kind of mental constipation which impedes this is one of the most important things to avoid.

(5) Contrasting with this is a kind of superficial fluency which impedes rather than assists the flow of thought, by obscuring it with a flow of words. There are people who do not take kindly to the sort of debate which our subject-matter demands, but who are only too eager to make long speeches or deliver wordy opinions about it. Asked to map out part of a town, they march confidently and rapidly down what they take to be the main streets, without either noticing the side roads or wondering whether what they take to be the main streets really are so. This is a tiresome and unconstructive method, and the rewards of it are meagre. Fluency in this sense belongs more to political orations or advertising than to the analysis of concepts.

(6) Finally, and perhaps more often observed than any other difficulty, there is the desire to moralise. Many words act as emotional stimuli for many people, in the sense that over and above their usage in ordinary language they carry with them implications of value.

Thus, to take obvious examples, 'Communism' and 'democracy' have a minus and a plus value respectively for most people in the western world: we might say, the one wears horns and the other wears a halo. More subtly, 'science' may imply for one man the march of progress, a brighter future, a sensible and down-to-earth approach, etc.: for another the horrors of atomic war, the inhumanity of machines, cold and unfeeling calculation, and so on. There are in fact few concepts to which our approach is not to some extent subjective and prejudiced. As a result there is a perpetual temptation to use and deploy these concepts as weapons rather than analyse them as subject-matter: we need only consider the amount of time spent in saying something good or bad about Communism compared with the time spent in saying something about the nature of the concept of Communism.

We could extend this list considerably but it may be more helpful to distinguish a common factor which runs through all our difficulties. All of them are essentially failures in *communication*. The analysis of concepts is a rather sophisticated form of communication: there are few, if any, fixed rules: and we have to learn how to proceed, as we have seen, in the same way that we learn how to play a game, or how to get on with people—by actually *doing* it as much as by learning the rules. We have, as it were, to have faith in the game: to throw ourselves into it with attention and alertness, but without too much anxiety. We have to be concerned, and eager to succeed, but not worried: controlled, but not inhibited. Some people err on the one side, and are not sufficiently concerned: they think that the whole thing can be easily settled, or that a speech by them will show everybody the complete answer. They are thus out of touch with the real situation: able to orate for their own benefit, but unable to communicate with others, unable properly to join in the game (like a football player who never passes the ball to anyone else). Others are too anxious and worried: feeling lost, and unable to cope with the situation at all, they remain silent and prefer not even to try (like a player who prefers not to touch the ball at all, and if virtually compelled to do so, passes it immediately to someone else).

Behind the notion of 'how to analyse concepts', therefore, there lies the still more general skill, 'how to talk' or 'how to communicate': and to employ this skill we have to learn above all to recognise and enter into the particular game which is being played. Thus the person who yields to the desire to moralise, who cannot talk *about* concepts but only preach *with* them, is essentially not playing the game: it is a form of cheating. Similarly the person who insists on analysing every single concept referred to in a statement is, so to speak, overplaying the game: like a soccer player who insists on dribbling skilfully in front of the goal when he should be taking a shot at it. To communicate, then, involves recognising the particular game and playing it wholeheartedly.

People often think that the analysis of concepts is a difficult game to recognise and play. The truth is, in my view, that it is difficult to recognise, but easy to play: that is why we have spent some time in trying to explain just what sort of a game it is. Here again it is rather like learning to swim: the chief difficulties consist of 'getting the feel' of the water—and ultimately in coming to realise within oneself the fact that the water will actually sustain one's body. Once one has done this, the whole scene changes, and swimming seems easy. It is as if there were a sort of click in one's mind, and one suddenly saw what the whole thing was about. Similarly in learning how to analyse concepts, you are asked to play a new game—to look at words from a new angle, to make a kind of mental twist: and after a certain amount of struggling, you see the point. Such struggling may not be very long or arduous, just as some people take naturally to swimming; but others may require time to get the necessary confidence. Nor are those who ultimately become the best swimmers necessarily those who took easily to the water at first.

Naturally people's temperaments differ: and my chief object in this section is to draw attention to the sort of difficulties experienced by everybody: that is, the difficulties experienced in learning a new game, in learning how to communicate in a new way. That is why I have spoken so often of analysing concepts as a game: not because it is not a serious and important matter, but because being like a game it is *not* like memorising a set of facts, or like trying to be more virtuous, or persuading people to vote for you, where the difficulties are quite different. With this in mind, and with the help of a little alertness and self-awareness, we may find it much more easy to avoid the mistakes which most of us make when we first try to analyse concepts: mistakes, indeed, which until very recently prevented human beings from playing the game of analysis consciously at all.

## B. *Techniques of analysis*

First, there are some general considerations which are nearly always of use to us, and which we should remember to apply whenever we are faced with any question which might seem to involve conceptual analysis:

### (1) *Isolating questions of concept*

We must begin by isolating the questions of concept from other questions. It is only rarely that one is presented with a question of concept in a pure form. Thus it is possible but unlikely that one will be asked a question like 'What is the logical nature of the concept punishment?': nearly always one is asked a more confused and complex question, such as 'Should people in mental asylums ever be punished?' Here one is being asked to play several different games, as it were. To answer the question in full it is necessary (i) to analyse the concept of punishment, (ii) to have some factual knowledge of what sort of people actually are in mental asylums, and (iii) to express some sort of moral opinion about whether punishment should be applied to these people. In other words, this is a mixed question, involving not only conceptual analysis, but also considerations of fact, and considerations of value as well. To take other examples, consider first the question 'Is freedom important for an individual in society?' Here we have a question in which both conceptual analysis and a judgement of value are called for: we need (i) to analyse the concept of freedom, and (ii) to express an opinion on its importance and its worth. Again, take the

question 'Is progress inevitable in the twentieth century?' Here conceptual analysis and factual considerations are both involved: we must consider the concept
of progress (and perhaps the concept of inevitability as
well), and then look at whatever facts concerning the
twentieth century we consider to be relevant.

It is not within our scope to consider how questions
of value or questions of fact should be answered. But it
is plain that we shall not answer any sort of question
very well (and certainly not a question of concept)
unless we distinguish very clearly between the logical
types of question that may be concealed within what
looks like a single question. There is only one question
mark, perhaps, but several questions: and we cannot
do any of them justice until we have dealt with each
of them separately. Obviously, to use the above examples, we cannot begin to say who should be punished
until we know clearly what punishment is: otherwise
we shall not know (in a quite literal sense) what we are
talking about. We need to understand freedom before
being able to express any intelligent opinion about
whether it is important, and progress before we can say
whether it is inevitable. We must, therefore, isolate the
questions of concept and give them priority.

## (2) '*Right answers*'

Closely connected with this is the point, already
made above, that questions of concept often do not have
any single, clear-cut solution. We are by now used to
the opening move 'It depends what you mean by...':
and this has important consequences for answering the
'mixed' questions described above. Briefly, its effect is

that *the whole 'mixed' question* has no 'right answer'. Thus we need not enter into a detailed analysis to perceive that we might well answer the 'mixed' question 'Is progress inevitable in the twentieth century?' by saying, in effect, 'Well, if you mean so-and-so by "progress", then (in view of certain facts) it is inevitable: but if you mean such-and-such, then it isn't'. Or to take another example, if one is asked 'Is democracy a satisfactory method of government?', one would begin by listing a number of uses or criteria for the concept of democracy, and then say something like 'Well, if you want to tie the word "democracy" down to *this* set of criteria' (which might involve, say, insisting that a country's budget should be balanced by popular vote rather than by acknowledged experts if the country is to count as a democracy), 'then in that sense of "democracy" it's obviously not very satisfactory, because it makes for instability: but if you only insist that the government should be elected by popular vote from time to time for the country to count as a democracy, then that seems quite satisfactory'.

This is one of the reasons why, as we saw above, it is important not only to isolate the questions of concept from other considerations, but to deal with them first: because considerations of fact and morality cannot be relevantly applied at all until one has worked out just what they are supposed to be applied *to*. When a 'mixed' question is asked, of the general form 'Is so-and-so (a concept) such-and-such (good, bad, inevitable in the twentieth century, etc.)?', the answer must sometimes be given in the form 'If by so-and-so you mean *abc*, then yes, because...: but if you mean *xyz*, then no, because...'. The examples concerning progress and democracy above should make this clear.

On the other hand, though we have seen that it is misleading to speak of '*the*' meaning of a word, it is equally mistaken to suppose that most concepts are completely fluid and can have more or less what limits one likes. We know of any concept that it occupies an area which can be roughly located and mapped, even if the frontiers are not in all cases very precise. Thus even if we may be in doubt as to whether whales, octopuses, starfish, lobsters and oysters fall inside the territory of the concept 'fish', we know at least that under most circumstances herrings, soles, plaice, trout, etc., certainly do. Moreover, there is a reason (or a set of reasons) why we are in doubt about whales and octopuses but not about herrings and soles: and this is because the concept 'fish' is not just an arbitrary concept, chosen for no particular purpose. Human beings find it necessary to have a word to describe things that satisfy certain conditions—being able to live in the sea, being living things rather than rocks or shells, being able to swim (unlike sea-anemones), and so on. Of course these criteria are to some extent vague. Do they include, for instance, what the creature *looks like*? Has it got to have fins and a soft body to count as a fish? If so, we have to exclude lobsters and octopuses. But then, what about jellyfish? They haven't got fins but they do have soft bodies; and besides, we do call them jelly*fish*. By thinking in this way we try to find out which of the conditions are important or essential, and which are inessential.

Thus we must not think either that we can say

definitely what a word 'really means', or that we can choose what it shall mean entirely to suit our own or someone else's convenience. In other words, some instances of the concept—some cases in which the word is used—are nearer to the heart of the concept than others. For instance, suppose we are examining the concept of truth. We might think of three instances of the word 'true': the case in which we talk of a statement or a belief being 'true', the case in which we talk of 'a good man and true' or 'a true friend', and the case in which we talk of a ball on a billiard table 'running true'. It is not hard to see that the first case is nearest to the heart of the concept. It is *primarily* statements and beliefs which are true: and though we can talk of 'a true friend', or of 'running true', or of 'true north', we could reasonably say that these uses were extensions or alterations of the primary uses—just as when we talk of the wind 'whispering' through the trees, we use 'whisper' as an extension of its normal use, a metaphor borrowed from its ordinary use as applied to people. By practice, you should be able to develop a kind of instinct which will enable you to distinguish the primary and central uses of a concept from the derived and borderline uses. It is this sort of sensitivity that makes all the difference between a useful and successful analysis and a clumsy attempt to analyse the concept merely by listing its instances without distinguishing between them.

We should now be in a position to see the use of other specific techniques of analysis:

## (3) *Model cases*

One of the best ways to start, particularly if we feel completely lost in the territory of a concept, is to pick a model case: that is, an instance which we are absolutely sure is an instance of the concept, something of which we could say 'Well, if *that* isn't an example of so-and-so, then nothing is'. Thus if we are considering punishment, we could take the case of a person who wilfully broke an important rule and was made to suffer for it at the hands of the authorities: say, a boy who deliberately broke a window in the school and was beaten by his headmaster. This, if anything, is certainly a case of punishment. We can then look at the features of the case and try and see which are the essential features in virtue of which we can and do correctly use the word 'punishment' to describe it. We might consider whether it is the fact that he broke a rule, or that he deliberately broke a rule, or that he was dealt with by the authorities, or that he was dealt with painfully, or some combination of these. Then we could take other model cases—say, someone who steals and is 'punished' by the sentence given by a judge in the law court—and see if all the features we noticed in the first case are also present in the second. If they are not, it might look as if the absent features are not essential: for if they were essential, they would perhaps[1] be present in *all* model cases. Thus we

---

[1] Perhaps, but not necessarily. There are some concepts which do have essential features: thus I doubt if we would ever count something as a box unless it could contain things. But there are others which do not have essential features in this sense, though they may have typical features: thus it is typical of cows that they have horns, and typical of games that they are activities in which two or more people can play; yet these are not essential features, for you can have a cow without horns,

can narrow down our search for the essential features by eliminating the inessential ones.

### (4) *Contrary cases*

We can do the same thing by an opposite method, taking cases of which we can say 'Well, whatever so-and-so is, *that* certainly isn't an instance of it'. Thus suppose we were worried about the concept of justice: we pick some cases where we would definitely want to say that someone was being treated unjustly. For instance, suppose an innocent person is sentenced to death for a crime he did not commit: or suppose two people commit the same crime under the same circumstances, and one gets punished but the other is let off. These are classic cases of injustice: and we then look at them to see why they are classic cases. Thus in the second example, where the law treats two people differently, it looks as if the essential feature is inequality of unfairness: is it because the people are not treated *the same* that we call the case 'unjust'? But then we might think of another contrary case: suppose two people both commit murder, but under different circumstances. Smith, a rich but greedy man, murders his victim simply to get a bit more money. Brown, a generous man who loves his wife, finds her in bed with another man: the man mocks him, Brown loses his temper and murders him. Both of these cases count as murder: but would it count as unjust if Smith were

and a game of solitaire or patience. In other words, some concepts refer to things which may not have any single feature in common, but which are linked by a group of characteristic but not essential features. With these, then, we must be content to look for *typical* features rather than *essential* ones.

condemned to death and Brown were only sentenced
to ten years' imprisonment? No, it wouldn't: but then
why not, since two people who committed the same
crime are being treated differently? What other circumstances do we have to take into account, in order to
be able to call a case 'just' or 'unjust'? Is it that Smith
*deserves* a worse punishment than Brown? Perhaps we
must now take some more contrary cases and learn from
them in the same way.

(5) *Related cases*

It is not often that one can analyse a concept without
also considering other concepts which are related to it,
similar to it, or in some way importantly connected
with it. Thus it is plain that we could not think very
long about punishment and justice, when considering
model cases and contrary cases as we have just done
above, without running up against the concept of
deserving: a concept which is in fact an essential feature
of its related concepts punishment and justice. Just as
one cannot understand one part of a machine without
at least a rough knowledge of how it fits into other parts,
and how those other parts work, so it is difficult to
grasp one concept without seeing how it fits into the
network or constellation of concepts of which it is a part.
So, in this example, it would be useful to see under what
circumstances we would be prepared to say that a
person 'deserved' to be treated in a certain way, and
when by contrast we would say his treatment was 'undeserved'. (We could do the same with the similar
concept of merit.) When we are clear about the criteria
for applying the related concept (deserving), it may

then be much easier to get clear about the original concept (punishment or justice).

## (6) *Borderline cases*

It is also helpful to take precisely those cases where we are *not* sure, and see what we would say about them. Suppose a child touches an electric wire which he has been told is dangerous, and then gets a shock: is the shock 'punishment'? It has some features in common with model cases of punishment, but perhaps not enough: and we then look to see which is the important feature that is missing. Is it perhaps that there is no *person* who gives the punishment? Then we might think of the case when we talk of a boxer 'taking plenty of punishment': are we serious in using the word 'punishment' here, or are we using it as a metaphor? Then what about someone like Macbeth in Shakespeare's play, who acted wickedly and suffered for it—can we say that 'he brought his own punishment upon himself'? Or is this also a metaphor? Then what about forfeits at Christmas parties, when someone fails to answer a riddle and has to pay a forfeit (by being made to eat some soap or put his face in a bowl of flour)? Are forfeits really punishments, or are they a sort of joking version of punishment, a play-acting of punishment? The point of all these cases is to elucidate the nature of the concept by continually facing ourselves with different cases which lie on the borderline of the concept: what we might call *odd* or *queer* cases. By seeing what makes them odd or queer, we come to see why the true cases are not odd or queer, and hence what makes them true cases—what the central criteria of the concept really are.

(7) *Invented cases*

Sometimes it is necessary to invent cases which are in practice quite outside our ordinary experience, simply because our ordinary experience does not provide us with enough different instances to clarify the concept. Thus there are lots of cases we can use to investigate punishment: but if we were investigating the concept of man we should find it hard to think up enough varied instances, because in the world as it is we rarely have any reason to hesitate about whether to call something a man or not. In practice men are sharply and easily distinguished from machines, apes, vegetables and so on. However, if we want to find out the essential criteria for the concept, we have to face ourselves with other cases, which will necessarily be imaginary and remind us more of science-fiction than real life. Thus suppose we discovered creatures hundreds of miles below the earth's surface which looked more or less like men, and had intelligence, but had no emotions, no art, and never made jokes. Would we count them as men? Or suppose they behaved just like men, with human emotions and all the rest, but had two heads? Or suppose we managed to build or grow a creature which was, say, more intelligent than a very backward pygmy and which laughed, wept, sometimes behaved angrily, at other times made jokes, and so on? Would that be a man, or would we disqualify it simply because we had built it or made it grow by artificial means? Of course, since these cases are so imaginary, we may well be in doubt about what we should call such creatures: but the exercise in imagination is useful for understanding our actual experience. For the analysis of concepts is essentially an imaginative process: certainly it is more of an art than a science.

## (8) *Social context*

Since language is not used in a vacuum, we must beware of thinking and talking as if questions involving general concepts were usually asked in papers set for examinations: in fact they are usually asked in everyday life, under the pressure of particular circumstances. The nature of these circumstances is very important for understanding the concepts. Hence we need to imagine, in the case of any statement, *who* would be likely to make such a statement, *why* he would want to make it, *when* he would most naturally make it, and so forth. Thus we might be faced with the question 'Are people ever responsible for their actions?' One good way of starting to get a grip on the concept of responsibility is to pick a practical case. Who would want to say 'This man is not responsible for his actions'? Well, let us say, a barrister defending a murderer in a court of law. He would want to say it because he wants to prevent his client being punished, perhaps: he would say it when it was clear that the man had done the murder, but when he thought there was a chance of the jury declaring him insane or irresponsible. The result of his gaining the point would be that the man would now not be treated so much as a wicked criminal but as an unfortunate patient, as someone suffering from a disease. This suggests that responsibility goes with guilt, the liability to punishment, and other related concepts.

(9) *Underlying anxiety*

Closely connected with the importance of looking at the social context of a question or statement is the importance of considering the mood or feelings of the person who makes it. Conceptual or philosophical questions often arise because of some underlying anxiety: certain features of life seem somehow to threaten the way in which we had always thought, and hence give us a feeling of insecurity. For instance, the question 'Are we ever really free?' may well be asked because many people have the feeling that modern psychology, by discovering more and more about the reasons for human behaviour, in some way threatens our freedom. Then they ask questions like 'Isn't perhaps *everything* that we do determined by some psychological factor in our own minds?' or 'Are we ever really free?' The underlying anxiety here consists in the feeling that, whereas hitherto one had felt *in control* of one's actions, now one is not so sure: and this is useful to notice, because the notion of being in control is important for understanding the concept of freedom.

(10) *Practical results*

Since conceptual questions are often misleading, in the sense that we cannot say without qualification that they have 'right' or 'wrong' answers, we may often wonder whether perhaps some such questions have any point or meaning at all. In fact, of course, since such questions are actually asked, they require some sort of answer: and in so far as people intend something by them, they have some sort of point and meaning. But sometimes we can only make a guess at the point and meaning: and one of the ways in which we can make our guesses intelligent rather than wild is to see what the practical results, in everyday life, would be if we answered 'Yes' or 'No' to the question. For instance, supposing someone asks 'How can we know that everything isn't an illusion?' or 'Is the whole of life just a dream?' It seems to make no practical difference how we answer. Suppose we said that everything was an illusion, or the whole of life was a dream. What of it? Would it affect our behaviour at all? Would it make any actual difference to what we did? Surely not: and this suggests that the question (though it may have some point or meaning) does not very well represent in words the underlying worry or doubt in the questioner's mind. In other words, something has gone seriously wrong with the language in which the question is put: for to any genuine or useful question it will make some practical difference which answer we give. Thus we can see in this example that, since the concepts *illusion* and *dream* only make sense at all in contrast to the opposing concepts *reality* or *waking life*, it is not clear what sense, if any, can be attached to saying that '*everything* is a dream' or '*everything* is illusory'. It would be like saying that *all* money is counterfeit. Having seen this, we then have a chance to guess more sensibly at what the questioner is really worried about: perhaps, for instance, he has found that some things, which he thought were real, were actually illusory, and this leads him to wonder whether everything is illusory. This is like the example in (8) above, where one learns that what one thought was a free action is in fact a compul-

sive one, and hence enters into a more general worry
about whether any action is free. As a result of such
questions we are led to consider very common concepts
(freedom, reality, etc.) in order to regain our security
and settle our doubts. If we start by a sensible and
down-to-earth consideration of the practical results of
answering these questions with a 'Yes' or a 'No', we
can then see which concepts the questioner is really
worried about.

## (11) *Results in language*

Since words are not used without ambiguity, and it is
not always possible to say what '*the*' meaning of a word
is, we may often be left with the situation described in
(2) above (page 25): that is, a situation in which we
have to say 'Well, if you mean *abc* by so-and-so, then
the answer is this: but if you mean *xyz*, then the answer
is that'. But we can, in fact, go further than this. For
even where words are so vague that they cannot be said
to have a central meaning, it is still possible to say that
it is more sensible or useful to adopt some meanings
rather than others. Thus the word 'democracy' has
very little central meaning: certainly, it has something
to do with the idea of the people exercising some control
on the government, but we cannot say very much more
than that. We could give various instances to which the
term 'democracy' has been applied: say, Athens of the
fifth century B.C., the United States in the last century,
Britain in this century, or even the 'people's democracies'
behind the iron curtain. In all these the people exercise
some control, so that all the examples qualify for inclu-
sion in the concept of democracy. But plainly, if the

word 'democracy' is going to be any use in our language, we want it to do as much useful work as possible. Thus it would be useful to have a term to contrast with 'totalitarian'—to describe a state in which the people can oppose the authorities without too much restriction. Hence we might wish to tie down the word 'democracy' in such a way that it excluded Soviet Russia (assuming Soviet Russia to be 'totalitarian' and restrictive in this sense), but included Britain. If we do not do this—and there is, in a sense, nothing to force us to do so—we should only have to invent another word to contrast with 'totalitarian'. Similarly we could say that in no state does the people really exercise *enough* control over the government for us to call the state truly democratic: but then we have tied down the word so tightly and restricted it so severely that it does no work for us: for now we do not allow ourselves to call any state a democracy—we have banned the word from our working vocabulary. In this way we have to look at the 'results in language' when choosing meanings for words or delimiting areas for concepts: we have to pick the most *useful* criteria for the concept. Thus, when (but only when) we have analysed the concept and noted the whole wealth of possible instances of it, we may often have to say at the end 'Amid all these possible meanings of the word so-and-so, it seems most sensible and useful to make it mean such-and-such: for in this way we shall be able to use the word to its fullest advantage'.

These techniques should become clearer when we come to apply them to instances of analysis: and I shall

refer to them specifically when we go through some
examples. Meanwhile it is worth noting that not all of
them are equally useful in all cases. When analysing one
concept we may find that there is not much point in
investigating the social context, or the practical results,
or the underlying anxiety: these may either be obvious
or irrelevant, or both. Thus if we were investigating
some abstract or academic concept, like the concept of
infinity in mathematics, or the concept of the subjunc-
tive in grammar, social considerations are not to the
point: certainly, we can say that to elucidate these
concepts would help mathematics and grammar, which
in turn would help our educational system, which in
turn would improve our society, but all this is not immediately relevant. By contrast, the meaning of a word
like 'good' may admittedly not be as simple to elucidate
as the meaning of 'fish', but we should not have to take
many model cases, borderline cases, etc., of the concept
of goodness to get a fairly clear idea of it. It is more
important to consider how the word 'good' is used
amongst people living in a society: for it is a common
word, and its actual meaning is not governed by any
very complex set of formal rules (in the way that
'infinity' in mathematics is so governed). On the
other hand, the social contexts in which it is used, the
practical results of using it in certain ways, and the
underlying anxieties about ultimate values, ideals, and
so forth are both complex and important.

In practice, the wisest course is to begin by applying
the techniques in order. Start by taking model cases,
contrary cases, related cases, borderline cases, and if
necessary invented cases: after one has worked for a

time on these lines, the actual rules governing the application of the concept should become reasonably clear. After that one can consider the social context, the underlying anxiety (if any), the practical results, and the results in language. As we have seen, not all of these may be useful in all cases, but it will always be worth while applying the technique and seeing whether it is likely to lead anywhere. After a reasonable amount of practice, one acquires a sensitivity towards the concepts which enables one to make the best use of the relevant techniques.

## C. *Pitfalls in language*

It is well known that in the course of discussion, reading, writing, or making any kind of statement we become aware of certain pitfalls in the use of language. Some of the more obvious of these are common knowledge, and come under the general heading of 'clear thinking': how to avoid fallacies, how to recognise prejudice, and so on. For our purposes, however, it is more important to stress the pitfalls that occur in more subtle forms. We fall into them for one general reason: because we are dominated and bewitched by language. Instead of using language, we are in a very real sense used by it: we allow words to guide our thinking, instead of guiding our own thinking consciously and critically. Just as psychoanalysis is intended to free us from domination or bewitchment by our own emotions and feelings of which we are unaware, so the analysis of concepts teaches us to avoid the pitfalls of language which are only dangerous because we are unaware of them.

(1) *Belief in abstract objects*

This is an elementary pitfall, but one which is very difficult to avoid: it seems to be ingrained into our way of thinking and hence into our language. We tend to think as if abstract nouns—particularly those which are connected with strong feelings on our part, like 'justice', 'love', 'truth', etc.—are the names of abstract or ideal objects: as if there were somewhere, in heaven if not on earth, *things* called 'justice', 'love' and 'truth'. Hence we come to believe that analysing concepts, instead of being what we have described it to be, is really a sort of treasure hunt in which we seek for a glimpse of these abstract objects. We find ourselves talking as if 'What is justice?' was a question like 'What is the capital of Japan?', instead of being a concealed demand for the analysis of the concept justice. Most of us (and here I exclude certain philosophers) do not feel tempted to say that there is an abstract thing called 'triangle' or 'symmetry' or 'redness': but with moral concepts in particular we yield to the temptation only too easily. It is a good though rather stringent working rule, at least when we are beginning, to use abstract nouns as little as possible: to *look at the uses of* 'just', 'true', etc., and not *look for* 'justice' or 'truth'. The belief in abstract objects is part of a general temptation to regard words as things, rather than simply as conventional signs or symbols (which is what they are).

(2) *Confusion between fact and value*

We have already noticed ((1) above, page 23) that there are such things as 'mixed' questions: that is, questions which demand both conceptual analysis and a value judgement, as 'Should people in mental asylums ever be punished?' But words as well as questions and statements are 'mixed' in this sense. Some words ('good', 'ought', 'right') can sometimes carry nothing but an expression of value, their sole function being to approve, condemn, praise, blame, etc.: other words ('honesty', 'stealing', 'noble', 'just') carry both factual meaning and also an implication of value: other words again ('natural', 'normal', 'mature') carry only a factual meaning in one of their senses, but in another carry an implication of value as well. Thus 'good' means 'to be approved' or 'commendable': 'stealing' means 'taking property legally another's' plus an implication that this is to be condemned: and 'normal' means either 'what most people do', or else 'what most people do' plus the implication that this is to be approved. It is extremely easy to introduce an implication of value unconsciously into a statement: and whilst of course judgements of value, if they are called for, are perfectly acceptable, one must remain clear about the point at which one introduces them.

## (3) *Unseen implications*

Some words beg the question in subtle ways: that is, they carry implications which one must not accept if one is to answer the question fairly. Thus the question 'If nature is well-ordered, must there not be a God?' can only be adequately answered if we first observe that the word 'ordered', like the words 'planned' and 'designed', normally implies a person who has done the ordering (or planning or designing). Of course one can speak, loosely but still correctly, of something being well-ordered or planned or designed without implying any such person: it is in this sense, perhaps, that all of us who marvel at the wonders of nature would agree that it is 'well ordered'. It matters little which sense we adopt: in the first sense of course it necessarily follows that there is someone who did the ordering (call it God if you like), because that is part of the meaning of that sense of the word: but then we want to ask whether nature *is* well ordered in that sense, i.e. whether we have to assume the existence of a God; so that nothing has been gained.

## (4) *Tautology*

When defending their opinions, people frequently try to make their statements safe by reducing them to tautologies: that is, to the sort of statement that is necessarily true because the speaker has made it true by definition. Thus, suppose we were trying to answer the question 'Do all Shakespeare's tragedies have villains in them?' We might start off by thinking of Iago in *Othello*, Edmund in *King Lear*, and so on, and form the opinion that the right answer is 'Yes'. If someone then says 'Oh, but what about *Julius Caesar*, or *Antony and Cleopatra*?' we may find it tempting to safeguard our opinion by making it tautological. We could do this in two ways. Either we could say 'Oh, they aren't really tragedies', or else we could say 'Well, Antony in *Julius Caesar* and Cleopatra in *Antony and Cleopatra* are really villains'. Now we may have other grounds for saying these things—other criteria for excluding the two plays from the concept 'tragedy' or for including the two characters within the concept 'villain': but (in this case at least) it hardly seems likely. If anything is a tragedy, surely *Julius Caesar* is: and Cleopatra and Antony are not villains in the sense that Iago and Edmund are villains. Probably our motive is simply that we wish to keep our opinion safe. But there is no point in doing this, since all we are now saying is really 'I shan't count anything as a tragedy unless it has a villain', or else 'If I count something as a tragedy, I shall insist that someone in it is a villain'. This is cheating: but more important, it is of no particular interest to anybody. It is easy to answer questions in any way you choose if you are allowed to monopolise words and give them your own meanings.

## (5) *Stretching the meaning*

There is no law against extending the normal meanings of words, but it is a dangerous procedure: and here again, we often feel tempted to adopt it in order to defend some particular point of view. It becomes fatal, however, when we stretch the meaning so far that the word ceases to do any work at all. For instance, suppose we face the question 'Do all novels have a political message?' We could tackle this in at least three ways. Perhaps the sanest way (i) would be to keep both feet on the ground, and recognise that normally we restrict the word 'political' to a few novels only: amongst these we might include Huxley's *Brave New World*, Orwell's *Animal Farm* and *1984*, and so on. But we might decide (ii) that we could stretch the word 'political', or at least the phrase 'have a political message', to cover more ground than in (i). Thus we could include C. P. Snow's *The Masters* on the grounds that, in describing the election of the Master of a college, it gives us insight into 'political' methods (obviously in a wider sense of 'political'): or we might even say that some novel about characters in the field of big business, in describing their immorality, greed, etc., carried an anti-capitalist message and was in that sense 'political'. But if we were to say (iii) that the novels of Jane Austen, P. G. Wodehouse and Iris Murdoch, together with the stories of Hans Andersen, A. A. Milne and Lewis Carroll, carried a political message, then the word 'political' has been stretched so far that it does no work, and becomes meaningless.

## (6) *Magic*

Finally there are a great many mistakes, not mentioned in the paragraphs above and impossible to list fully, which (as we said earlier) are basically due to our being bewitched or dominated by a form of language. When we make these mistakes, we are nearly always thinking (usually unconsciously) in a primitive or childish way, as if we believed in magic instead of believing in what we observed or learnt by reason. The belief in abstract objects ((1) above) is one instance of this, but only one. For example, in a statement like 'gravity made the stone fall downwards' the danger is not only that we might believe in an abstract *thing* or *force* called 'gravity' (whereas in fact all we really observe is various objects behaving in regular ways): the danger is also that we may take the word 'made' too seriously. The stone was not compelled to fall: it just fell, as stones and other things always do when they are near some large body of matter. When we say things 'obey' the 'laws' of nature, we are talking magic: talking as if nature and natural objects were people, or as if there were little men inside the objects with wills of their own. This tendency to magic, deeply inbred into our thinking, used to cause endless trouble in the early days of science: and it now causes just as much trouble when we face problems connected with people —problems of morality, psychology and so on.

## D. *Style*

The style in which we express our analyses of concepts, or our answers to conceptual questions, is immensely important. For it is not just a matter of what style of speech or writing looks or sounds nice, but of what style best fits the subject-matter: and for this activity above all others, to choose the wrong style is to handicap oneself in its performance. It is totally impossible, for instance, to set down a clear and sensible analysis of a concept if you are trying to be rhetorical, magniloquent, or epigrammatical.

On the other hand, it is important—even if it is not demanded of you for an examination—to set out your analysis on paper, in as final and coherent a form as possible. Not till you do this, or at least are fully prepared to do it, can you see the weaknesses and gaps in your analysis: thoughts and ideas which might seem lucid and complete in your head come to seem muddled and fragmentary once you think of actually putting them down on paper. The process of expressing your thoughts—again, particularly in this activity—assists the thoughts themselves, and acts as a kind of filter or governor for them. Hence it is very valuable to grasp the sort of style, the mode of expression, which is suited to the analysis of concepts: if only because, by imitation and practice of the style, the analysis itself becomes easier and more efficient.

So far as the literary qualities of the style go, there is little to be said. The only important criterion is that it should be *workmanlike*. This, of course, involves being above all clear and straightforward, not tortuous, obscure or irrelevant: it involves being economical in your words, though not so miserly that the reader is in any doubt about your meaning: and naturally it involves making good use of paragraphs, punctuation and so on—a particularly important feature in writing a conceptual analysis, since the use of grammatical devices like punctuation is to gain greater logical clarity, and such clarity is the be-all and end-all of this activity. Avoid rhetoric, epigrams, quotations (unless directly relevant and enlightening), and all other literary devices of that nature: but make full use of any device which is logically illuminating. Thus analogies are often helpful to get across a particular logical point: but any kind of high-flown language ('purple passages', poetic metaphors and the like) is dangerous.

Perhaps the most important quality which you should seek after in writing, however informally, about concepts is the quality of *honesty*. Anyone who deliberately tries to obscure a point for his own ends, or is content to draw a conclusion which he knows quite well does not follow from what he has said earlier, is of course doomed from the start: but there are more subtle and involuntary forms of dishonesty which are harder to detect and rectify. It is helpful, when one is just about to write something or has just written something, to ask 'Do I *really* mean this?', 'Is this *really* what I intend to say?', or 'Is this *really* true?' Since the business of analysis is essentially a dialectical business, no statement can possibly be perfect and complete, and in that sense no statement is ever entirely satisfactory. But one can gain an increasingly firm hold of the truth by continually forcing oneself to become conscious of the imperfection of one's own statements: by realising that they need qualification, that there are points to be made that might upset them completely, and so on.

This is the real reason, perhaps, why high-flown or tortuous language is to be avoided: it obscures, not only for your reader but for yourself, the point that you are trying to make. The merit of a simple and lucid style is not just that it is easier to read: it is that mistakes are more easy to detect, and hence more easy to rectify. There is a close parallel here with one's behaviour towards other people. If you are honest and straight-forward in your dealings with other people, you gain not only the advantage that other people know where they are with you, but also the greater advantage that you know where you are with them: that is, you know how you really feel towards them, because you have not covered up your real feelings by trying to act dramatically, or by being oversubtle and dishonest, or by attempting to be too clever. To be honest means to be direct, clear, straightforward, and at the same time

continually aware of what one is doing or saying—
continually trying to make one's intentions and feelings
match one's deeds or words. This is a difficult process,
but immensely rewarding.

In the following sections of this book I shall give some
examples of conceptual analysis: some illustrations of
how to criticise passages written by other people, of the
sort of internal and informal dialogue you need to
conduct with yourself, some 'model' answers to conceptual questions, some notes on the logic of certain
interesting concepts, and so on. I want to insist very
strongly that you should not regard either the style or
the content of these as in any sense 'ideal'. Whether
you agree or disagree with what is said is not the most
important thing, just as it is not important whether the
'model' answers really are model. (Obviously in at
least one sense they cannot be, since there is no end to
what one could say about most of the concepts, some of
which lie at the root of philosophical problems of great
complexity.) If you disagree with them and back up
your disagreement by making points of your own, or if
you can observe logical flaws and superficialities, or
even if you think that there are radical and systematic
errors, so much the better. What really matters is the
*general method of approach*. In the analysis of concepts
there is no 'complete answer', but only a number of
logical sketches of greater or less merit. To remember
this may have the doubly useful effect of preventing you
from striving arrogantly after the impossible, and en-
couraging you to make a logical sketch of your own
which will contribute something worth while. A philosopher who thinks he has nothing at all to say on a

subject is either unnecessarily despairing, or just lazy: and a philosopher who thinks he has said the last word on a subject needs to think again.

### 3. ADDITIONAL NOTES

There are two topics relevant to this chapter and to the book as a whole. Both are rather complicated; and since I do not think them essential to the understanding of the book, it would be wise for anyone who finds them difficult or confusing to omit them at this point, and return to them later. I have put them here, however, because they are chiefly relevant to this particular chapter.

### A. *A title for the techniques*

It might help the reader to give the techniques we are discussing a name; and to consider what name to give them might improve our grasp of what the techniques are like. In other words, though there are difficulties in naming the techniques, we may be able to turn these difficulties to advantage by seeing in what ways the techniques are like other 'subjects', and in what ways unlike.

Thus to call the techniques 'logical thinking', would be in some ways informative and in some ways misleading. Certainly they are concerned with thinking— like most mental techniques: and certainly they are concerned with thinking 'logically'. But of course the concept of logic or logicality is just the sort of concept we have described above—a puzzling concept whose geography needs to be mapped more exactly. For instance, one might take 'logically' to refer to what is normally called 'formal logic'. This is indeed a 'sub-

ject', defined originally by Aristotle, concerned with
the rules and procedures of formal arguments such as
'All men are mortal: Socrates is a man: therefore
Socrates is mortal'. But whatever the importance of
this subject, it is not ours: our techniques are much
looser, more informal, less precise—indeed 'informal
logic' would not be a bad title for them, though it would
not at first sight be a very comprehensible one. Other
people, faced with the phrase 'logical thinking', might
regard this as just another way of saying 'straight
thinking' or 'clear thinking'. This too, though perhaps
not a clearly defined 'subject' like formal logic, is
certainly something which books are written about: in
such books one might expect to be told to avoid prejudice, to keep one's temper, to look out for fallacies in an
argument, to check the facts, to keep to the point, and so
on. But to translate 'logical thinking' by 'clear thinking'
might mask the fact that 'logical' can mean far more
than just 'reasonable' or 'clear': for as we have seen,
there are certain new and specific techniques dealing with
words, meanings, verification, concepts and criteria—
techniques which it is reasonable to call 'techniques of
logic' rather than just 'techniques of reasoning'. Neither
formal logic, then, nor 'clear thinking', give us a satisfactory idea of what we have called 'logical thinking'.

In the same way we might be tempted to describe
the work done by such techniques as essentially the
work of philosophy. But the concept of philosophy is
also a puzzling concept and one which is very much in
dispute at the present time. It would be misleading in
this context, because it includes far more than our
techniques. It includes, to name but one activity, the

giving of general advice on how to live one's life (such as might be offered by a 'guide, philosopher and friend'): and this is no part of our task. Certainly our techniques are widely and effectively used amongst modern philosophers, particularly in England and America: there is every reason to think them very important for philosophy in any sense of the word, and even to believe that anyone who wants to study philosophy should begin by mastering them. But to describe the techniques briefly as 'elementary philosophy' would be trying to gain an unfair monopoly of the concept of philosophy.

Plenty of other names and titles could be considered and rejected. What about 'the analysis of general concepts'? This is a fair enough description, but like many descriptions that are tolerably exact it gives little indication of its subject-matter: it achieves exactitude at the price of being incomprehensible. Or 'how to use words'? Again this is a fair description, but only in a sense: the description could be applied just as fairly to a book about English grammar or one designed to increase one's vocabulary, or even one designed to improve one's powers of debating and public speaking. Even something like 'the meaning of words' will not really do: for this might describe a book about the derivations and root-meanings of words in different languages—a book which told you that Kaiser and Shah and Czar all came from the Latin word 'Caesar', for instance.

The truth is that there is no description of these techniques which is at once brief, accurate and comprehensible. Either you pick a phrase which is accurate but not comprehensible to the layman ('logical analysis' or 'the analysis of general concepts'), or one which looks comprehensible but which may be very misleading ('clear thinking' or 'the use of words'). This is because these techniques are not widely practised, at least consciously: though one could say that a good deal of unconscious struggling with concepts takes place, even in everyday life. The reasons for this in turn are various: partly it is because the techniques (or at least their conscious application) are fairly new; partly because those who use them—the people who have taught or learned philosophy at certain universities in the last two or three decades—have not been very much concerned in spreading their use more widely; and partly because there is a good deal of psychological resistance to taking such techniques seriously and learning to acquire them. These conclusions may appear unhelpful and discouraging: but they should serve, at least, as a warning not to try to assimilate the techniques to other 'subjects' with which we may be more familiar—to pretend, for instance, that they are 'just a matter of defining your terms', or 'just clear thinking'. There is a perennial temptation to do this, but it is fatal to yield to it. Like most techniques that are really worth anything, they are not really like anything else except themselves: just as a game may have similarities with another game, but cannot be played properly unless it is accepted on its own merits and in its own right.

However, the techniques with which we are concerned do derive from the kind of philosophy which has been practised at Oxford, Cambridge and elsewhere in England and in America for about thirty years. This is often fairly (though again incomprehensibly) described as 'linguistic philosophy' or 'linguistic analysis'. The techniques in this book may be regarded as borrowed, watered-down, developed, advanced, simplified, over-simplified or what you will, when considered in relation to the techniques of linguistic philosophy: that hardly matters. But the point may be helpful for those who wish to place our techniques in some sort of logical or historical setting. Linguistic philosophy is the activity most nearly approximating to our own: and those who are concerned to pursue this point further may find the remarks in the last chapter of this book helpful.

## B. *What is a concept?*

In this chapter I have spoken as if questions of concept and questions of meaning were identical: thus I have said that the question 'Is a whale a fish?' is a question about the concept of a fish, and said also that it is a question about the meaning of the word 'fish'. I have also spoken, somewhat indiscriminately, about 'our idea of a fish', 'how we use the word "fish"', and so on. In doing this I have been trying to be comprehensible rather than precise: and the distinction I have chiefly aimed at clarifying is the distinction between questions of concept and meaning on the one hand, and other questions (questions of fact, questions of moral opinion, and so on) on the other. However, in doing this I inevitably ride rough-shod over the distinction between concepts and meaning: and since this may worry some readers, I must try to say something about this distinction here. Anything I say, however, will be very tentative: for we are here up against some tough philosophical problems.

The first thing to say, perhaps, is that just as there is, strictly speaking, no such thing as 'the' meaning of a word, so there is no such thing as 'the' concept of a thing. When we talk, in a kind of shorthand, about 'the' meaning of a word, we refer to those significant elements in all the many and various usages of the word which make the word comprehensible, to the area of agreement amongst users of the word. In the same way when we talk of '*the*' concept of a thing, we are often referring in an abbreviated way to all the different concepts of that thing which individual people have, and to the extent to which these concepts coincide. Thus we can talk about 'the' concept of justice entertained by the ancient Romans; but also we can talk about your concept of justice, or my concept, or Cicero's concept, just as we often say '*His* idea of justice is so-and-so'. We must not, in any case, imagine that 'the' concept of a thing is a separate entity on its own.[1]

Next, let us consider briefly how we come to form concepts. Human beings at a very early age learn to group certain features of their experience together, and to use certain words to describe these groups. Thus a child, having first sorted out his sense-experience into numbers of separate entities or objects, begins to discriminate between one sort of object and another. He may, for instance, wish to put all large objects with

---

[1] Wittgenstein compares the notion of family resemblances. Different members of the same family may look alike, so that we can sensibly talk of 'a family resemblance': but they do not necessarily have one specific feature in common. Of course they *may* have something, like a Habsburg nose: but very often the resemblance consists of a general likeness, and there is nothing we can point to in particular.

flat tops into one group. As soon as he does this, he begins to form a concept. In this case, his concept may be approximately similar to an adult's concept of those objects which we call 'tables'. But the child might make mistakes: if he simply groups together everything with a flat top, he will include what we call pianos and sideboards. There are two ways in which he may adjust his concept. First, he may finally observe that only certain flat-topped objects are used for serving food on, and cut down the limits of his concept accordingly; and secondly, he may learn the use of the word 'table' from adults. This learning of the word 'table' may proceed in two ways also. First, he may do it by trial and error: he points to the piano and says 'Table', and some adult says 'No, *that's* not a table: *this* is a table' (pointing to a table). Secondly, if the child can talk and understand properly, it can be explained to him what a table is by the use of other words: thus an adult might say 'Tables are what you eat off'. In the same way, someone who did not know what a tiger was, someone who had formed no concept of a tiger, could be taught in two ways. Either you could take him to the zoo, point to each animal in the tiger-house and say ' *That's* a tiger, and that, and that', and then, taking him round all the other houses in the zoo, 'but not *that*, or that, or that'. This would be a very arduous and uncertain method: though, if you showed him things that he might naturally mistake for tigers (jaguars, leopards, tabby cats, etc.) and diligently said 'No, not that', he would probably get a fair idea of a tiger in the end. The second way could be used if he understood enough words for you to say to him 'Tigers are four-footed wild animals, quite like domestic cats only bigger, with stripes and long tails'.

From this we can see that concepts and meaning are very closely connected: the processes of forming a concept of a thing, and of learning the meaning of a word which describes the thing, may often look like the same process. But in fact they are not. It is quite possible to have a concept of something, but for there to exist no single word—not even a word invented by the person who has the concept—which describes the thing. Thus I might have a very clear idea of the sort of dog I want to buy, or the sort of girl I find attractive, or the sort of atmosphere I think is common to certain ghost stories, without having one particular word to describe these things. I might do my best, in communicating with other people, by saying 'I want a *man's* dog', or 'I like *vivacious* girls', or 'M. R. James's ghost stories have a sort of *unexpected spookiness*'. But none of these words might get very close to delineating those features which I wish to delineate: there may be no words which do neatly delineate them, though no doubt in principle it would always be possible to invent words and teach them to other people.

This also shows that one can have a concept without having a mental image or picture of anything. To many people it is often helpful if they can form a clear picture of something, and perhaps as children some of us may start on the business of forming concepts by being able to picture objects even when they are not directly before our eyes. But though I might (and probably would) picture my special sort of dog and girl, I am unlikely to picture my special quality in certain ghost stories—yet it might still, in some sense, be very clear in my mind: I might be very much aware of it and very certain about whether a particular ghost story had this quality or not. Indeed it is plain that concepts of justice, together with other abstract concepts, need not be attached to any pictures at all. When I think about justice, or when someone utters the word 'justice' in my hearing, I may indeed form a picture—for instance, I may picture the statue of Justice outside the Old Bailey, with a sword in one hand and a pair of scales in the other. Someone else may picture a bewigged judge, another man a policeman, and so on. But these are accidental associations: though, of course, we may cling on to them so hard that they muddle our thinking and our talking. It would be possible, for instance, for a young child to derive his concept of a tree solely from one immense oak in his back garden. If he continued to retain such a narrow idea, we should say that his concept was a very limited one, and that he must have had a very limited experience of trees; and if he used the word 'tree' in reference only to the limited concept, we should say that he did not really understand what the word meant. But the mere fact that he should entertain the picture of his special tree *whilst* using the word might be purely accidental: it would be evidence neither of his having a very limited concept of trees, nor of his having a properly formed concept like other people.

As we have noticed, our use and understanding of a word are closely related to our concept of a thing. We form concepts by learning the uses of words, and it can be seen what concepts we have formed by seeing what we understand by words: putting it another way our

use and understanding of language act both as guides
to forming concepts, and as tests of concepts when
formed. Thus we could truly say that the logical limits
of a concept may be the same as the limits to the range
of meaning of a particular word: for instance, the limits
of a man's concept of justice are the same as the limits
within which he uses and understands the word
'justice'. This is not to say that the concept and the
meaning are identical: but it is to say that they are, as
it were, parallel to each other, or that they cover the
same logical area. So long as we are only concerned
with the logical range of a concept, then the best
possible guide is the logical range of the word with
which the concept is normally associated.

When we talk in this book, then, in such phrases as
'the concept of justice', and then go on to examine
different uses of the word 'justice', we should now be
able to see that seeking the justification for these uses is,
in fact, analysing the concept of justice. On the one
hand there are a number of situations in real life (boys
being punished, judges giving sentences, and so on): on
the other a word, 'justice', which is used in different
ways. Using both these sources, each of us forms a
concept of justice: and to analyse this concept is to
present ourselves with different uses of the word in
different real-life contexts. We are thereby as it were
reliving the time when we came to form the concept—
presenting ourselves over again with actual situations,
in imagination, and considering the propriety of the
use of the word 'justice' in relation to these situations.

Finally, if we are to answer the question 'What is a
concept?', we must allow a certain degree of arbitrari-

ness in our reply. Our only interest in this context is with what we might call the logical aspect of concepts— their limitations and applications: and these can be analysed linguistically. But it could plausibly be said that a concept, as the word is normally used in English, can be viewed psychologically as well as logically. We might, after all, be interested in what sort of pictures, if any, a person had, or how sharply delineated they were, or in whether a man's concept of justice was entertained with emotional or moral force. All these points might reasonably feature in answer to a question like 'What is your concept of Germans?': I might reply, for instance, 'Nasty blond men with whips and Gestapo uniforms, unpleasantly efficient and industrious'. This would be a perfectly fair reply, even though it might not correspond at all with my understanding and use of the word 'Germans'—I might understand and use the word in exactly the same logical way as people who were less prejudiced against Germans than myself. This is of some importance to our purpose, since only too often people do take these accidental psychological connotations of their concepts with logical seriousness—just as I might allow my conceptual prejudice to influence my use of language when talking about Germans, refusing to count nice Germans as Germans at all. Since this book is not primarily concerned with such conceptual prejudice, however, we need not worry too much about this point: we can be content to note that it is difficult to draw a clear line of demarcation between the logical features of a concept and its psychological connotations, and continue with our task of investigating the logical features.

## CHAPTER II

# EXAMPLES OF ANALYSIS

### I. CRITICISM OF PASSAGES

One of the best ways of getting practice in the analysis of concepts is to see how concepts are used or abused by other people: and in this chapter we shall give some passages which need the special kind of conceptual criticism that we have been investigating. Here again it is worth repeating that this criticism is not a matter of formal logic, nor a matter of 'straight thinking' merely. It is only rarely that we can, on the one hand, convict the authors unhesitatingly of a classic fallacy of the sort found in textbooks on logic: but on the other hand it is inadequate to say that the passages are just 'confused', or 'obscure', or that the author 'hasn't defined his terms', or 'is prejudiced'. What happens in these passages is that concepts are mishandled: or to speak more precisely, handled without full awareness and clarity.

Hence it is conceptual criticism that is needed: and the methods of analysis discussed in chapter 1 should prove equally helpful here. Instead of merely letting ourselves be carried along by what the author writes, or alternatively of rejecting the whole passage out of hand, we must try and penetrate beneath the words to the way in which the concepts are handled. We must have sufficient sympathy with the author to realise just what is happening to the concepts: it is rarely that authors talk sheer nonsense, and there is usually some plausibility in what they say. On the other hand we must maintain enough critical alertness to react immediately, when we find that the concepts are being distorted.

We shall take, first, two longish passages of dialogue —one from the fourth century B.C., and the other from our own century—and secondly, some short passages from various authors: on both I shall make some logical comments of a fairly informal kind.

## A. *Plato's 'Republic'*

This passage is a translation of part of Book I of the *Republic*; I have left out some bits, because they merely hold up the argument. Socrates is describing the dialogue in the first person: hence the 'I' in this passage means Socrates. His opponent, Thrasymachus, speaks first:

'Listen, then,' he said. 'I define justice or right as what is in the interest of the stronger party.'

'You must explain your meaning more clearly,' I said.

'Well, then, you know that some states are tyrannies, some democracies, some aristocracies? And that in each city power is in the hands of the ruling class?'

'Yes.'

'Each ruling class makes laws that are in its own interest—a democracy democratic laws, a tyranny tyrannical ones, and so on; and in making these laws they define as "right" for their subjects what is in the interest of themselves, the rulers: and if anyone breaks their laws he is punished as a "wrongdoer". That is what I mean when I say that "right" is the same thing in all states, namely the interest of the established ruling class; and this ruling class is the strongest element in the state, and so if we argue correctly we see that "right" is always the same, the interest of the stronger party.'

'And are those in power in the various states infallible or not?'

'They are, of course, liable to make mistakes,' he replied.

'When they make laws, then, they may do the job well or badly.'

'I suppose so.'

'And if they do it well the laws will be in their own interest, and if they do it badly they won't, I take it.'

'I agree.'

'But their subjects must obey the laws they make, for to do so is right.'

'Of course.'

'Then according to your argument it is right not only to do what is in the interest of the stronger party, but also the opposite.'

'What do you mean?' he asked.

'Did we not agree that when the ruling powers order their subjects to do something, they are sometimes mistaken about their own best interest, and yet that it is right for the subject to do what his ruler orders?'

'I suppose we did.'

'Then you must admit that it is right to do things that are *not* in the interest of the rulers (who are the stronger party): that is, when the rulers mistakenly give orders that will harm them, and yet (so you say) it is right for their subjects to obey those orders. For surely, my dear Thrasymachus, in those circumstances it follows that it is right to do the opposite of what you say is right, since the weaker are ordered to do what is against the interests of the stronger.'

'A clear enough conclusion,' exclaimed Polemarchus.

'No doubt,' interrupted Cleitophon, 'if we are to take your word for it.'

'It's not a question of my word,' replied Polemarchus, 'Thrasymachus himself agrees that rulers sometimes give orders harmful to themselves, and that it is right for their subjects to obey them.'

'But,' objected Cleitophon, 'what Thrasymachus meant by "the interest of the stronger" was what the stronger *thinks* to be in his interest: that is what the subject must do, and what was intended by the definition.'

'Well, it was not what he said,' replied Polemarchus.

'It doesn't matter, Polemarchus,' I said. 'If this is Thrasymachus' meaning, let us accept it. Tell me, Thrasymachus, was this how you meant to define what is right—that it is that which seems to the stronger to be in his interest, whether it really is or not?'

'Certainly not,' he replied, 'do you think that I call someone who is making a mistake "stronger" just when he is making his mistake?'

'I thought,' I said, 'that that was what you meant.'

'That's because you're so malicious in argument, Socrates. No craftsman or scientist ever really makes a mistake, nor does a ruler so long as he is a ruler: though it's true that in common parlance one may talk about the doctor or the ruler making a mistake, as I did in what I was saying just now. To be really precise, one must say that the ruler, in so far as he is a ruler, makes no mistake, and so infallibly enacts what is best for himself, which his subjects must perform. And so, as I said to begin with, "right" means the interest of the stronger party.'

*Comments*

(*a*) Thrasymachus starts off by saying 'I *define* justice or right as...'. He is offering a definition of the word: or so he claims. But is he really doing this? If so, he is wildly astray. A definition is some word or phrase which is linguistically equivalent to what is being defined—a translation, as it were, of one word into others. (Thus *triangle* equals 'a three-sided figure in two dimensions': *puppy* equals 'young dog', or 'dog that has not yet grown up'. Wherever one can use one phrase one should be able to use the other.) Now look at Thrasymachus' 'definition'. Could anyone seriously imagine 'the interest of the stronger party' to be *linguistically equivalent* to 'right'? Obviously it isn't: for one thing, if it were equivalent, we should never be able to say 'This is in the interest of the ruling class, but I don't think it's right', whereas in fact we can and do properly say things like this. 'Right' just doesn't mean what Thrasymachus says it does.

(*b*) Well, then, what is he doing? Perhaps he is just saying that the ruling classes make the laws, and that they always make laws which benefit themselves. If so, this is a statement of fact: we should naturally turn to the historian or sociologist to tell us how far it was true. It may indeed be both true and important: but how far does this sociological point have anything to do with the meaning of 'right'?

(*c*) Perhaps he is trying to say 'What most people actually call right is, in fact, what the ruling classes ordain' or more precisely 'If the ruling classes ordain so-and-so and such-and-such, then it's these actions and this sort of behaviour that most people will call "right"'. The idea here is, that if you want to know what things are actually called 'right', or what makes them 'right', then you would do well to look at the things which are in the interest of the ruling classes, because they co-incide: and they coincide, of course, for the very good reason that the ruling classes make laws and establish moral codes in their own interest, and it is by virtue of these laws and codes that people call things 'right'.

(*d*) If Thrasymachus' sociological point in (*b*) above is true, is (*c*) then also true? Let's take a parallel. You might ask the question: 'What is "a good boy" in a school?', and say 'Well, "a good boy" is the sort of boy who satisfies the demands of the educational establishment: the boy who makes no trouble, does his work conscientiously, perhaps plays a leading part in games and other activities, is obedient, and so on: in other words, the sort of boy who serves the interests of the establishment or the ruling classes (the masters)'. This is to admit (*b*), that the establishment lays down rules in its own interest; and also to admit (*c*), that when people talk of 'a good boy' (as on a school report, for instance) they usually mean the sort of boy who serves the interests of the establishment. But we still don't want to say (see (*a*) above) that 'good' *means* 'serving the interests of the establishment': it obviously doesn't mean that, even though 'a good boy' may mean a boy who serves the interests of the establishment. This looks queer.

(e) It now looks as if, towards the end of (d) above, we have been using 'means' in two different ways. Suppose we try saying 'A good boy does, in fact and in practice, really mean a boy who serves the interests of the establishment': and then '"Good" means "serving the interests of the establishment"'. The first is plainly true, the second false. This should show the two different ways in which 'mean' can be used:

(i) as 'linguistically equivalent to';
(ii) as 'in practice identifiable with'.

We can see these two uses if we imagine a general saying 'We need something more powerful than conventional weapons', and another general answering 'That means the atomic bomb'. 'Means' here is used in sense (ii) above: nobody would imagine that the phrases 'the atomic bomb' and 'something more powerful than conventional weapons' were linguistically equivalent.

(f) In any case, as we saw in chapter 1 (page 41), moral words of general application such as 'good' and 'right' are primarily used to approve or commend, and hence cannot be linguistically equivalent to any such factual phrase as 'the interests of the stronger'. Even though the actual things that people in practice may call 'good' or 'right' may be of a certain kind, we cannot tie down the use of 'good' or 'right' to things of that kind only. We *can* always say 'Well, even if he does serve the interests of the establishment and hence would normally be called "a good boy", I don't think he's

really a good boy'; or 'Even if most people call it
"right", I don't think it is'. So we should hesitate
before admitting (c) above. If Thrasymachus is saying
'What people call "right" usually is, in practice,
identical with what is in the interests of the ruling
classes', then (provided he is right about the facts) we
could admit this. But we would not want to admit that
'right' *means* this, not at least without going carefully
into how 'means' is used here.

(g) How is this sociological point—the point that
laws and moral codes, in virtue of which people call
things 'right', are laid down for the interest of the
authorities—affected by what Socrates says? Thrasymachus has the choice between adopting Cleitophon's
suggestion and rejecting it. He can either say:

(i) 'Right' boils down to what the authorities say
is right, even if they sometimes say things that don't
serve their own interests; or else

(ii) 'Right' boils down to what is really in the
interests of the authorities, whatever the authorities may
say.

Thrasymachus appears to adopt the first of these, but
in effect adopts the second. For if we amend the first to
something like 'and the authorities always do say what
serves their own interests (otherwise we won't count
them as authorities)', the first in effect becomes the
second. Imagine the headmaster of a school who lays
down rules. Then a word like 'well-behaved' comes to
mean (in one sense of 'mean') 'obedient to the headmaster's rules'; and if we add that the headmaster
makes rules in his own interest, then we can say that
conduct which is well-behaved boils down to conduct

which is in the headmaster's interest. But now suppose the headmaster gets drunk and makes some wild rule, such as a rule that all boys must have at least one love affair with a local girl every term. This isn't in his interest, because it will get him into trouble with the school governors, the education authorities, the parents, and so on. Now, what shall we say is 'well-behaved' conduct *vis-à-vis* this rule? If we take Thrasymachus' line, we say that when he made the rule he wasn't really acting as headmaster: so that the 'well-behaved' boy would disregard the rule, as not being really in the headmaster's interests. Alternatively we could say that the 'well-behaved' boy would, as usual, be obedient to the rules, including this rule.

(*h*) The general sociological point, that behaviour which most people think to be 'well-behaved' (or 'right', or 'just') is in general that behaviour which is in the interests of the authorities, is valid. Sometimes the authorities are not the best judges of their own interests, and then it's a matter for further discussion whether we adopt Cleitophon's suggestion or not: but the point still stands.

(*i*) Thrasymachus' last speech looks odd. We should naturally be inclined to say, 'If Thrasymachus admits that "in common parlance one may talk about the doctor or ruler making a mistake", why isn't he satisfied with this? What's the point of going into this curious conceptual contortion, whereby he says that "the ruler, in so far as he is a ruler, makes no mistake"?' But it would be wrong to think that Thrasymachus talks in this way just because he is trying to avoid the edge of Socrates' criticism: he cannot be assumed to

be a fool, and he could equally well have avoided it by adopting Cleitophon's suggestion. His concepts, therefore, must be different from ours. To him, so it seems, the art or science comes first and its practitioner second, whereas with us it is the other way round. We believe, first and foremost, in a doctor: and then we would agree, if pressed, that there is some skill or expertise which doctors often use, well or badly. Thrasymachus believes primarily in an expertise called 'curing people': and 'doctor' is conceptually defined (at least strictly speaking) only in terms of this expertise. In other words, a 'doctor' is someone engaged in 'curing people'; and therefore, by strict definition, when he isn't curing people he isn't a doctor. Thus he isn't a doctor when he makes mistakes about medicine or is on holiday. Plainly we have here a quite different constellation of concepts from our own.

## B. *A modern dialogue*

This is a dialogue between Bertrand Russell and Father S. C. Copleston, S.J. The complete debate was originally broadcast by the B.B.C., and dealt with the existence of God. I have here extracted a passage which concerns morality and judgements of value.

RUSSELL (1). I feel that some things are good and that other things are bad. I love the things that are good, that I think are good, and I hate the things that I think are bad.

COPLESTON (2). Yes, but what's your justification for distinguishing between good and bad or how do you view the distinction between them?

RUSSELL (3). I don't have any justification any more than I have when I distinguish between blue and yellow. What is my justification for distinguishing between blue and yellow? I can see they are different.

COPLESTON (4). Well, that is an excellent justification, I agree. You distinguish blue and yellow by seeing them, so you distinguish good and bad by what faculty?

RUSSELL (5). By my feelings.

COPLESTON (6). By your feelings. Well, that's what I was asking. You think that good and evil have reference simply to feeling?

RUSSELL (7). Well, why does one type of object look yellow and another look blue? I can more or less give an answer to that, thanks to the physicists, and as to why I think one sort of thing good and another evil, probably there is an answer of the same sort, but it hasn't been gone into in the same way and I couldn't give it you.

COPLESTON (8). Well, let's take the behaviour of the Commandant of Belsen.[1] That appears to you as undesirable and evil, and to me too. To Adolf Hitler we suppose it appeared as something good and desirable. I suppose you'd have to say that for Hitler it was good and for you it's evil.

RUSSELL (9). No, I shouldn't go quite so far as that. I mean, I think people can make mistakes in that as they can in other things. If you have jaundice you

[1] Belsen was a German concentration camp in the 1939–45 World War, where many atrocities were committed by the Commandant and others.

see things yellow that are not yellow. You're making a mistake.

COPLESTON (10). Yes, one can make mistakes, but can you make a mistake if it's simply a question of reference to a feeling or emotion? Surely Hitler would be the only possible judge of what appealed to his emotions.

RUSSELL (11). It would be quite right to say that it appealed to his emotions, but you can say various things about that: among others, that if that sort of thing makes that sort of appeal to Hitler's emotions then Hitler makes quite a different appeal to my emotions.

COPLESTON (12). Granted. But there's no objective criterion outside feeling, then, for condemning the conduct of the Commandant of Belsen, in your view?

RUSSELL (13). No more than there is for the colour-blind person who's in exactly the same state. Why do we intellectually condemn the colour-blind man? Isn't it because he's in the minority?

COPLESTON (14). I would say because he is lacking in a thing which normally belongs to human nature.

RUSSELL (15). Yes, but if he were in the majority, we shouldn't say that.

COPLESTON (16). Then you'd say that there's no criterion outside feeling that will enable one to distinguish between the behaviour of the Commandant of Belsen and the behaviour, say, of the Archbishop of Canterbury.

RUSSELL (17). The feeling is a little too simplified. You've got to take account of the effects of actions and your feelings towards those effects.... You can

very well say that the effects of the actions of the
Commandant of Belsen were painful and unpleasant.

COPLESTON (18). They certainly were, I agree, very
painful and unpleasant to all the people in the camp.

RUSSELL (19). Yes, but not only to the people in the
camp, but to outsiders contemplating them also.

COPLESTON (20). Yes, quite true in imagination. But
that's my point. I don't approve of them, and I
know you don't approve of them, but I don't see what
ground you have for not approving of them, because
after all, to the Commandant of Belsen himself,
they're pleasant, those actions.

RUSSELL (21). Yes, but you see I don't need any more
ground in that case than I do in the case of colour
perception. There are some people who think everything is yellow, there are people suffering from
jaundice, and I don't agree with these people. I can't
prove that the things are not yellow, there isn't any
proof, but most people agree with me that they're
not yellow, and most people agree with me that the
Commandant of Belsen was making mistakes.

*Comments.*

(*a*) The passage as a whole is concerned with the
*justification* of moral judgements. But it doesn't seem
to make much progress: Copleston's demand for a
justification at the beginning (2) is echoed at the end
(20), and Russell's original answer (3) is also repeated
(21). It is possible that Russell's replies were completely
clear and satisfactory, and that Copleston just didn't
see the point, but this isn't very likely: and it's also
unlikely that Russell's answers were completely unclear

and unsatisfactory. Almost certainly the dialogue is inconclusive: and since it seems to go round in circles, perhaps something has gone wrong with it.

(b) We can begin by clearing away some irrelevancies:

(i) In 7, Russell isn't giving any kind of *justification* for his moral views: he is suggesting that there may be a scientific (presumably a psychological) *explanation* for them, just as there is an explanation why some things look yellow and blue.

(ii) In 4–6, Copleston introduces the idea of a *faculty* in virtue of which Russell judges things or distinguishes things as good or bad. The implication of 4 ('Well, that is an excellent justification') and 6 ('Well, that's what I was asking') is that asking what faculty is used is the same as, or importantly connected with, asking what justification can be given. But this isn't clear. One might use a faculty to collect evidence, but it's the collected evidence and not the mere use of the faculty which provides the justification. Thus one might use one's faculty of hearing, and thereby get an impression that there's been a certain kind of noise: but the justification for believing this would be the impression itself, the impressions of others, what was recorded on a tape-recorder, and so on. Anyway, has there *got* to be a faculty by which one distinguishes things? By what faculty does one distinguish true from false, happy from unhappy, pain from pleasure, beautiful from ugly, and so on? We could answer (like Russell) 'By our feelings', but does this help at all? It seems doubtful whether this concept is very useful: and perhaps it is fortunate that it is soon dropped in this dialogue.

(c) Now, does this parallel of Russell's between moral judgements and seeing colours really work? One would naturally suspect that it doesn't, since value-words don't function in the same way as descriptive words (chapter 1, page 41). We can in fact (contrary to Russell in 21) prove things to be yellow or blue: in saying that something is yellow, we are stating facts which can be verified by agreed methods. In this case, we should ask various other people whether they thought it was yellow: and ultimately we could measure the light-waves it gave off. But 'good' doesn't work like that. Since 'good' is primarily used to commend and not to state facts at all, we certainly shan't be able to prove that things are good in the same way that we can prove that they're yellow: indeed, perhaps we shan't be able to 'prove' that things are good at all (though obviously this depends on what we're going to count as 'proof').

(d) So Russell is wrong (13, 15 and 21) in suggesting that it's a matter of opinion merely whether we call something yellow or not. In answer to 13, we condemn the colour-blind person not just because he's in a minority, but because he is actually colour-*blind*: that is, as Copleston implies in 14, because he's deficient in some way—he can't distinguish colours that other people can distinguish. We can easily test this: for instance, the colour-blind person can't distinguish between the 'Stop' and the 'Go' on traffic-lights. He would be in this sense deficient even if he were in the majority.

(e) However, Russell dithers about this. In 9, he talks of 'making mistakes' about colours: and this doesn't make sense if he also thinks (21) that there 'isn't any proof' about colours. He seems similarly to dither about moral judgements. It is as if he were saying, on the one hand, that they need no justification —you just feel things to be good or evil, and that's the end of it—and, on the other hand, that you can make mistakes in your moral judgements (9, 21). He is obviously anxious, towards the end of the passage, *not* to say that there's no way of showing the Commandant of Belsen's actions to be evil: but he doesn't make it clear how he could show this. He could show (21) that most people, like himself, also felt them to be evil, but this doesn't prove anything. As he says, there isn't any proof along these lines. But then if there is no proof at all it doesn't make sense to talk about 'making mistakes'.

(*f*) Russell could have consistently maintained one position, the position that in making moral judgements one is simply expressing a feeling. This position might be crudely stated by saying that '"This is good" just means "I like this"'. It isn't very plausible, but it gets round the difficulty about the Commandant of Belsen. For if 'this is good' *just* means 'I like this', then there's no real *dispute* between Russell and the Commandant. The Commandant is just saying 'I like doing this sort of thing' and Russell is saying 'Well, I don't'. If both sides are just expressing their feelings, then there's nothing to dispute *about*. This would settle the point about justification: you don't need to justify moral judgements if moral judgements can be translated into 'I like this', 'Hooray for that!', 'Down with so-and-so!', and so on.

(*g*) Copleston is quite right in implying (20) that

Russell's efforts to justify his belief in 17 and 19 are useless. Russell could have taken the opposite line to the one just mentioned in (*f*) above, and held that some moral feelings were justifiable, for example, as he suggests in 17 and 19, by seeing whether most people thought some action to be unpleasant. He could have said outright '"Good" means "what most people think to be pleasant"', or something like that. In that case one could, of course, prove things to be good: you just find out what things most people think to be pleasant (which is a matter of hard fact), and there you are. Then you can talk of proof, making mistakes, justification and so on. But Russell won't do this—or at least not consistently. When he says things like (17) 'You've got to take account of the effects of actions...' and (19) 'to outsiders contemplating them also', he seems to be changing his mind. Why, if there's no question of justification or proof, has one 'got' to form one's moral judgements by looking at the effects of actions? Or why should one be concerned with what outsiders feel? To say this would only make sense if we could produce some reason why people *ought* to do these things, and this would only make ·sense if the whole business of moral judgements were supposed to be amenable to proof, justification and so on; and Russell has not shown this to be the case.

(*h*) However, the inconclusiveness and inconsistencies of Russell's position are significant, because they at least point to a genuine dilemma. On the one hand we don't see how we can sensibly talk of 'proof' and 'justification' in morals, since value-words don't describe facts: but on the other hand, we don't want to say that the whole thing is just a matter of taste. In other words, we want to be able to prove that the Commandant of Belsen's actions are bad—we're not content with just saying 'We don't like the way he acts': but we also see logical difficulties in the way of proving this sort of thing. Perhaps the answer lies in formulating a different notion of 'proof' or 'justification', a notion applicable to moral judgements and moral arguments even though it won't apply to arguments about facts. (This is one of the most serious problems—perhaps the most serious—in modern moral philosophy.)

## C. *Shorter passages*

### (1) *C. S. Lewis, 'Christian Behaviour'*

Some of us who seem quite nice people may, in fact, have made so little use of a good heredity and a good upbringing that we are really worse than those whom we regard as fiends. Can we be quite certain how we should have behaved if we'd been saddled with the psychological outfit, and then with the bad upbringing, and then with the power, say, of Himmler? That is why Christians are told not to judge. We see only the results which a man's choices make out of his raw material. But God doesn't judge him on the raw material at all, but on what he has done with it. Most of the man's psychological make-up is probably due to his body: when his body dies all that will fall off him, and the real central man, the thing that chose, that made the best or the worst out of this material, will stand naked. All sorts of nice things which we thought our own, but which were really due to a good digestion, will fall off some of us: all sorts of nasty things which were due to complexes or bad health will fall off others. We shall then, for the first time, see everyone as he really was.

## Comments

(*a*) We have here a picture of human beings as essentially consisting, not of what their heredity or environment or position in life make them, but as things that can make moral choices. When their heredity, etc., 'fall off' them, we shall see them as they 'really' are. People who 'seem quite nice' may be 'really worse' than, for example, Himmler. 'The real central man' is 'the thing that chose'.

(*b*) The most striking point is that, although this picture may be in keeping with what some of us believe (or profess to believe), it is not at all in keeping with the way we normally *talk*. Normally we count as part of a man features which can be shown to be greatly influenced, if not entirely determined, by heredity and environment: his intelligence, his good temper, his physical appearance, his sense of honour, and so on. We don't put these in the same category as things like his bank balance or the house he lives in: of these we're prepared to say that the man has been saddled with them, but of the things like intelligence we say that they are part of the man. Indeed, it's just these things which go to make up what we mean by the word 'man' or 'person'.

(*c*) If, following Lewis, we don't allow these to count as part of a man (or not 'really' part), we are left with 'the thing that chose'. We have disqualified everything that is due to heredity and environment—and however much of a man we think this to be, it is certainly going to be a very great deal: so that the remaining features (his will? his soul?) seem rather thin. Indeed, could one conceivably apply the word 'man' to a 'thing that chose'? Whatever this feature of man is, it is only one feature: and unless we are going to revise the concept 'man' radically, this one feature is not enough to call something 'a man'.

(d) Indeed, the whole notion of saying that what seem to be parts of a man really aren't, the whole picture Lewis presents, seems so difficult to conceive that we wonder if it is sense at all. Is there, in fact, a part of man which we can describe as 'the thing that chose', entirely separate from anything to do with his heredity and environment? Can we logically separate such a part? We should want to conduct a very careful investigation before agreeing to this picture.

(e) Moreover, if we did accept it, we should have to revise a large part of our language. At present it makes no sense to say that nice people may 'really' be worse than Himmler: for no meaning can be attached to the word 'really', unless we first accept the picture as a whole. This is one of those many passages where, despite the fact that the words used are common English and in themselves quite comprehensible, we are asked to accept a totally new picture of the world, and to face a totally new use of concepts.

## (2) *Aldous Huxley, 'The Doors of Perception'*

We live together, we act on, and react to, one another; but always and in all circumstances we are by ourselves. The martyrs go hand in hand into the arena; they are

crucified alone. Embraced, the lovers desperately try
to fuse their insulated ecstasies into a single self-
transcendence; in vain. By its very nature every em-
bodied spirit is doomed to suffer and enjoy in solitude.
Sensations, feelings, insights, fancies—all these are
private and, except through symbols and at second
hand, incommunicable. We can pool information about
experiences, but never the experiences themselves.

*Comments*

(*a*) To say 'We live together, but we are always by
ourselves' is paradoxical. It looks as though (chapter 1,
page 43) the limits of some concept are being stretched
too far. If we are always by ourselves, can any sense be
attached to the notion of being together with someone,
or sharing something with someone? Would Huxley
ever allow himself to say 'So-and-so is not by himself'?
This is something, after all, which we do say very often.
In other words, there are cases in life when we do want
to say (whatever words we use) 'This person is *not*
alone', or 'not in solitude', or 'not separated': and
why should we not say it in the words we have just
used?

(*b*) Presumably Huxley yields to the temptation to
stretch the concept of 'being by oneself' so far because
he wishes to make some point. What point? Perhaps
that we can never communicate our experiences 'except
through symbols and at second hand': or perhaps that
we can never 'pool...the experiences themselves',
that is, that we can never have the same experience as
another person. Let us look at these in order:

(i) To say that 'we can never communicate our

experiences except through symbols' is odd, because it implies in the context that there could logically be communication without symbols, but that in human life as it is there never is. But could there? Surely all forms of communication involve artificial signs or symbols (the words of a language, gestures, the Morse code, etc.): this is what 'communication' *means*. To say that we can never communicate except 'at second hand' is odd for the same reason. What would a case of communication at first hand look like? All communication is 'at second hand' in the undisturbing sense that it involves the mediation of symbols.

(ii) Is it worrying to say that we can never have 'the same experience' as another person? Obviously there is a sense in which this is true: Smith cannot have Brown's headache (though of course in another sense he can have 'the same headache', or the same sort of headache, as Brown). But to say that Smith cannot have Brown's headache is not to express a regrettable fact of nature that might be otherwise: it is to express a truth of logic. Smith cannot have Brown's headache because if Smith had a headache it would not be Brown's headache at all, but Smith's—it would be *nonsense* to say Smith had Brown's headache. It's like taking the phrase 'If I were you' seriously. Obviously I can't really be you—it's not sense: though of course I can put myself in your place, share your feelings, sympathise with you, and so on.

The implication of all this is that Huxley is lamenting, not something which is factually the case but might not be, but rather something which is a logical necessity. As long as we give sense to the distinctions marked by

words like 'I', 'you', 'Smith', 'Brown', etc., it necessarily follows that we have to think of these people and
their experiences as distinct and not as identical.
Naturally we can conceive of situations which would
give more weight to such phrases as 'communication'
or 'sharing experiences'—for instance, telepathy. But
this does not alter the main point.

(3) *Sir Arthur Eddington, ' The Nature of the Physical World'*
    I think we should not deny validity to certain inner
convictions, which seem parallel with the unreasoning
trust in reason which is at the basis of mathematics,
with an innate sense of the fitness of things which is at
the basis of the science of the physical world, and with
an irresistible sense of incongruity which is at the basis
of the justification of humour.  Or perhaps it is not so
much a question of asserting the validity of these convictions as of recognising their function as an essential
part of our nature. We do not defend the validity of
seeing beauty in a natural landscape; we accept with
gratitude the fact that we are so endowed as to see it
that way.

*Comments*
    (*a*) The first two sentences suggest different views.
It is one thing to talk of 'validity', 'convictions' and
'justification', and another to talk of things having a
'function as an essential part of our nature'. The former
implies that we are assessing *beliefs*, seeing whether
there is *evidence* to *justify* them, and so on: the latter
suggests that we are looking at human faculties or
behaviour-patterns, and considering how they work,

whether they are useful or 'essential', whether they are important cogs in the human machine. The last sentence seems to come down in favour of the second sort of talk rather than the first: we are to consider not the validity of human beliefs but the value of human endowments.

(b) Suppose we start by talking in the first way: this seems more natural if we are worried about 'certain inner convictions', since we may presume that a 'conviction' is a belief *that* something is the case. When dealing with convictions or beliefs, our prime interest is to know whether they are true: and for this purpose we are not interested in whether they are useful, comforting, or 'essential', nor whether they can be accepted with gratitude, but solely with whether they are reasonable, whether they are 'valid' or 'justifiable', whether there is enough evidence in their favour.

(c) Some beliefs are justifiable and others aren't. Eddington seems to think that mathematics, as a system of beliefs, isn't justifiable—that it depends on 'the unreasoning trust in reason': and he thinks that science depends on 'an innate sense of the fitness of things'. Without going deeply into the logical basis of mathematics and science, we can see that this looks odd. If the beliefs of mathematics and science aren't valid, what is? Surely the majority of these beliefs are the very models of what rational belief is supposed to be.

(d) As applied to humour, however, this sort of talk will not do: because humour doesn't involve any system of beliefs. Hence it would be logically out of place to talk about 'evidence', 'validity', 'justification' and so on.

(*e*) If we now move to the second sort of talk, then this now seems inappropriate because it isn't how we usually assess 'convictions', or sets of beliefs like those of mathematics and science—though it is more the way we assess activities like humour. In other words, we would justify humour by saying that it's pleasant, or psychologically useful: but we would justify beliefs by saying that they're true.

(*f*) Now let's look at the last sentence. If 'seeing beauty in a natural landscape' involves entertaining a *belief* (for example, the belief expressed in some such statement as 'That landscape is beautiful'), then we need the first sort of talk, the talk about validity, evidence, justification, and so forth. If it doesn't involve a belief but only a feeling (for example, the feeling expressed in 'Gosh, I love looking at that!'), then (as with humour) we needn't worry about truth: we need only worry, if at all, about whether the feeling is pleasant or useful.

(*g*) Finally, we can tie this up with the 'inner convictions' mentioned at the beginning. If Eddington means just 'feelings', then the passage as a whole is acceptable: but one suspects that he starts by meaning 'beliefs' and is concerned to justify these, and that he then suppresses the key point about justifying beliefs by evidence, ending up by imagining that 'inner convictions' *in any sense of the phrase* can just be 'accepted with gratitude' as part of our human endowment. But, in fact, some feelings conjoined with some beliefs may seem a basic part of our natures, yet be unjustifiable by any methods. Thus, religious feeling and belief may be of this kind, as also the feeling and belief that one belongs to a 'master race' and is for this reason entitled to murder and persecute people of 'inferior breeds'.

## (4)  *D. H. Lawrence, 'Edgar Allen Poe'*

It is easy to see why each man kills the thing he loves. To *know* a living thing is to kill it. You have to kill a thing to know it satisfactorily. For this reason, the desirous consciousness, the SPIRIT, is a vampire. One should be sufficiently intelligent and interested to know a good deal *about* any person one comes into close contact with. *About* her. Or *about* him. But to try to know any living being is to try to suck the life out of that being. Man does so horribly want to master the secret of life and of individuality *with his mind*. It is like the analysis of protoplasm. You can only analyse *dead* protoplasm, and know its constituents. It is a death process. Keep KNOWLEDGE for the world of matter, force, and function. It has got nothing to do with being.

### Comments

(*a*) It is very obvious that something funny is happening to the word 'know' here. Normally one says 'I know Smith very well' without any implication, either in logic or in fact, of 'killing' Smith or 'trying to suck the life out of him'. Lawrence is presumably aware of this common usage, but wishes to make some point which involves a distorted use of 'knowledge'. In other words, the distortion is so extreme that it may be deliberate. What point is he trying to make?

(*b*) He draws a distinction between (i) knowing things about Smith, and (ii) knowing Smith. (i) is all right, according to Lawrence, but (ii) is a vampire-like process, a process of trying to 'master' Smith with one's mind. It is a method of approach to Smith which is bad, because 'it has got nothing to do with being'. Obviously this method of approach is not the one we normally adopt when we say 'I know Smith' or 'Do you know London well?'

(c) There is a sense in which, when we are 'trying to get to know London' we are trying to 'master' it with our minds: presumably Lawrence does not object to this. But one can think of a sense in which one could try to 'master' a person with one's mind: for example, when one treats him as a psychiatric case, when one is grossly inquisitive and tries to dominate him, interfere with him, and as it were feed off him for one's own benefit. We can think, for example, of an over-possessive mother, and see that there is a sense in which we could say that she tries to 'know' her son too much, to 'master' him with her mind.

(d) We can then distinguish (i) cases of knowing people which are unobjectionable, and (ii) cases of knowing people which involve domination, possessiveness, or 'eating them up'. Lawrence calls (i) 'knowing things about' people, and (ii) simply 'knowing' them. Why does he want to distort and monopolise the word 'know' in (ii) for his own purposes? This is not easy to say simply in the light of the present passage: one could perhaps hazard a guess that he is anxious to contrast an intellectual, analytic or exploiting approach to people ('knowing' them) with other forms of approach—loving them, having physical contact with them, accepting them, communicating with them, and so on.

The distortion is misleading: but there may be a valid and important point behind it.

### (5) *Herbert Butterfield, 'Christianity and History'*

I must confess that if in the ordinary course of teaching I were to ask for what I should carefully call the 'historical explanation' of the victory of Christianity in the ancient Roman empire, I should assume that there could be no doubt concerning the realm in which the problem was to be considered, no doubt that I had in mind the question 'how' Christianity succeeded and not the more fundamental question 'why'. As a technical historian, that is to say, I should not be satisfied with the answer that Christianity triumphed merely because it was true and right, or merely because God decreed its victory. I remember taking part in a viva voce examination in Oxford over ten years ago when we were left completely and permanently baffled by a candidate who ascribed everything to the direct interposition of the Almighty and therefore felt himself excused from the discussion of any intermediate agencies.

### Comments

(*a*) The general force of this passage is that certain kinds of talk (talk about what is true or right, or talk about the will of God) are inadequate for 'historical explanation'. The candidate who presumably answered every question at the viva voce by some such remark as 'Well, it was the will of God' left the examiners 'completely and permanently baffled'. All this is immediately comprehensible.

(*b*) On the other hand, some of the qualifications in the passage are odd. Butterfield is careful to say that 'as a technical historian' he would 'not be satisfied' with the answer that Christianity triumphed *merely* because it was true or right, or *merely* because God decreed its victory. The implications are that it is only as a technical historian that he would not be satisfied: that as a technical historian he would have no objection in principle to the reasons given, but would find them unsatisfactory because inadequate (perhaps because they are not full enough?): and that *merely* to give these reasons is unsatisfactory, because there are other reasons which also ought to be given. In other words, Butterfield's objections seem to be two:

(i) the reasons are unsatisfactory as an answer to the question 'Why did Christianity triumph?' *if that question is regarded as a question of 'technical history'*;

(ii) they are unsatisfactory not so much because they are wholly out of place—the wrong sort of reasons altogether—but because they are not full enough.

(*c*) If we are correct in drawing these implications—and admittedly the passage is not long enough for us to be sure—then there is something funny about it. Surely we could say, about the objections above:

(i) To say 'Because God willed it' is unsatisfactory as an answer to the question 'Why did Christianity triumph?' in *any* sense of the question, or in any sense which we can think of. It's unsatisfactory because it doesn't *explain* anything: just as, if we asked 'Why did the Red Sea divide?' and were told 'Because God willed it' or 'It was a miracle', we should have been told nothing *by way of explanation*. For science, history, or any other subject which is supposed to explain things, answers of this kind are useless.

(ii) Thus it's not just a matter of the reasons being not full enough, but of their not really being reasons at all—or not explanations, anyway. As reasons, both in this context and any other context of explanation, they are quite out of place.

(d) It looks as if Butterfield hasn't seen this, because he says earlier 'I had in mind the question "how" Christianity succeeded and not the more fundamental question "why"'. This is an odd way of talking. Surely, when he sets examination papers, he does say things like '*Why* did Christianity triumph?'—it would be queer to say '*How* did Christianity triumph?' Surely 'why' *can* ask for an explanation: in fact, if we had to draw some distinction we might well say that 'why' asked for an explanation whereas 'how' asked only for a description. (Contrast 'Why does litmus paper behave as it does?' with 'How does litmus paper behave in acid?') So what is this curious distinction that Butterfield makes?

(e) Again, we can't be quite sure without looking at more of Butterfield's writing. But we could see how an answer like 'Because God willed it' *might* be an answer to 'Why did Christianity triumph?' if we use 'why' in a certain sense, to mean 'In fulfilment of what purpose?' or 'In fulfilment of whose purpose?' or 'By whose design?' (This would be like my saying 'Why did you sit down?' and your answering 'Because I wanted to, because I was tired of standing up'.) It is quite in order to ask such questions (though they may not have answers), provided we are clear about exactly what sense we are giving to 'why'.

(6) *John Wilson, 'Reason and Morals'*

We may mean by 'miracle' something which human beings will in practice never be able to explain (because it is too hard for them, as it were): or we may mean something which logically cannot be explained, which is by definition inexplicable. Believers in the ultimate inexplicability of human beings face a similar ambiguity. The motives for uncertainty are plain enough, since if they stick to the first sense, miracles become devalued: they are no more than phenomena which are very, very difficult to understand. They may be 'mysterious' in this sense, but in no other important sense. For we can, of course, conceive of circumstances which would enable us to understand a miracle or a human action: and without much difficulty, either.

*Comments*

(*a*) Wilson is here trying to impale those who believe in miracles on the horns of a dilemma. The dilemma is roughly this: Either events called 'miracles' are just events which are very puzzling and difficult to grasp (in which case we needn't worry because we may be able to grasp them in time), or else 'miracle' means 'an inexplicable event' or 'something no one could ever under any circumstances explain' (in which case it seems rash to say there are miracles, for how do we know that nobody will ever explain them?). This all seems very neat and tidy, but someone who really does believe in miracles is left with a vague feeling of having been cheated. Does the dilemma really work?

(*b*) A believer in miracles could deny that his position

is fairly stated by *either* alternative. Miracles aren't *just* 'events which are very puzzling and difficult to grasp': but at the same time one isn't satisfied with saying that miracles are 'by definition inexplicable'. Let's look at each of these in turn:

(i) Why aren't miracles *just* baffling events? Because we could draw a distinction between one sort of baffling event (say, the fact that the brain produces a certain type of rhythm when a man is sleeping) which isn't *in principle* baffling, but just very difficult to explain: and another sort (say, the dividing of the Red Sea) which somehow is *totally* baffling because it's the product of a higher intelligence (God) which we can't in principle understand.

(ii) Why don't we want to accept the phrase 'by definition inexplicable' without further discussion? Well, in a sense we might agree that acts of God were 'by definition' inexplicable—by definition, that is, of what one means by 'God' or 'human being', since you might define 'God' as a being whose acts couldn't possibly be understood by 'human beings'. But this conveys a very different impression from just saying that miracles are 'by definition inexplicable': for if you just say that, the implication is that they make no sort of sense whatever, whereas what we've just said suggests that they make sense to God but not to us.

(*c*) We might clarify this by an illustration. Imagine ants in an ant-hill, and assume them to have some sort of rudimentary intelligence. Then sometimes human beings do things which affect them: they pour boiling water on them, or save them from being eaten up by other ants, or they turn the ant-hill round so that it always faces the sun. Now we might say the ants can't, in principle (that is, because they are ants), grasp the explanation for these 'miracles'. They are, indeed, baffling events: but these baffling events are baffling in a higher order than baffling events like the invasion of another army of ants, or the rebellion of some slave-ants, or the sudden collapse of part of the ant-hill. Again, is it fair to say that the 'miracles' done by the humans are 'by definition inexplicable'? The logical position isn't clear. In other words, further discussion is needed to do justice to the case of the believer in miracles.

(d) This makes some of Wilson's remarks misleading, for example 'They may be "mysterious" in this sense' (that is, they may be very hard to understand) 'but in no other important sense'. But there is another important sense, exemplified by the illustration above: human acts are, it is suggested, baffling to ants in the important sense that they are *human* acts—they produce a quite different and greater order of bafflement. Again 'we can of course conceive of circumstances which would enable us to understand a miracle... without too much difficulty' is misleading, because it neglects the same point. The ants *could* conceive explaining some ordinarily baffling event (for example, a sudden fall of earth in the ant-hill), but surely it's possible to say that they *couldn't* conceive explaining, for example, the sudden pouring of boiling water on the ant-hill by humans.

(e) All this shows the danger of trying to eliminate all your adversaries at one blow. There may be people whose belief in miracles is not wholly dependent on their belief in a God who is beyond the range of human understanding, and who interferes with the world in ways which are in principle incomprehensible. For these people Wilson's arguments should carry weight. But for those whose belief in miracles hangs solely on a prior belief in a God of this kind, they are inadequate. In other words, the belief in miracles is part and parcel of a particular religious metaphysic, and can't be entirely destroyed without considering the metaphysic as a whole.

### 2. ANSWERING QUESTIONS OF CONCEPT

In this particular kind of conceptual analysis it is essential to adopt the right method of procedure, because you are going to end up with a formal and finished essay rather than just with a number of separate logical comments expressed in an informal way. At all costs, therefore, do not start writing at once, otherwise you will get into an impossible tangle, and probably want to contradict your first paragraph with your second. You may well feel that you have as much to say about a question of concept as the next man, so that you might as well start writing straight away: but this temptation must be resisted. To yield to it is unwise enough even when answering questions of other kinds, when it is fairly clear what points you are going to have to deal with. But with questions of concept it is quite fatal, because you do not even start by knowing what the relevant points are: there is no kind of framework round which you can build.

In order to make such a framework, you must somehow achieve a situation (before writing anything down) in which you have a number of points which you can make in order, issuing in some kind of conclusion and in as definite an answer to the question as can be managed. To do this I recommend the following procedure: a procedure which may sound clumsy, and parts of which may be skipped after some practice, but which it is as well to adopt in full when one is beginning:

(1) Act as advised in chapter 1, page 23: that is, isolate the conceptual question or questions from the rest of the question: write down the concepts to be analysed.

(2) Apply the techniques on pages 28–39 (model cases, contrary cases, etc.) to each concept, and see what light they shed upon it. Note briefly on paper any points which seem particularly significant.

(3) In the light of the previous step, conduct a kind of dialogue with yourself about the concept, in your head. Ask yourself questions and answer them: invent new cases when you feel like it: go back to the application of the techniques in the last step of the procedure if you wish. This sort of informal talk with yourself is one of the most important elements in the procedure. In the course of it you should observe what are blind alleys, and what points seem to lead somewhere: certainly you should have the basic outline of the concept properly clarified in your own mind by the end.

(4) Now take another look at the actual question. This may cause you to lay more stress on some points as particularly relevant, or to demote others as not bearing directly on the question.

(5) In the light both of your informal dialogue and

the question itself, list on paper the points you are going to make, and the conclusion you are going to reach.

(6) Write the essay point by point (though connecting up the points as far as possible).

(7) Finally, look back on what you have written, and emend any remarks that are obviously indefensible or extravagant (as well as emending any mistakes of a stylistic nature, such as bad grammar, punctuation, etc.).

Like all sets of instructions, this is apt to sound painfully slow: just as if one were to learn to swim by being told 'Place your right hand in the water in front of your head: keep the fingers together, and bring it back along your body as far as it will go, remembering to breathe meanwhile...' and so on. You feel that by the time you have carried out all these instructions you will have sunk to the bottom. But it is still not a bad way to start: and it is at least helpful in showing you what you have done wrong when you have actually written an essay, so that you can then pay especial attention to whatever part of the instructions you unconsciously failed to carry out.

We shall now take two questions and endeavour to answer them by the procedure laid down in the last section. I shall make frequent reference to the general considerations of analysis mentioned in the last chapter (pages 23–27), to the specific techniques (pages 28–39), and to the pitfalls of language (pages 39–45): the reader will find it helpful to refer to these sections when they are mentioned.

A. '*Ought punishment to be retributive?*'

*Step I*

We notice, first, that there are two concepts which are obscure: 'punishment' and 'retributive': and that these therefore require analysis. Secondly, we notice that the question 'Ought...?' implies that we may be called on to make a judgement of value. Consequently we decide to delay the judgement of value until we have analysed the concepts.

*Step II*

We now apply some of the techniques of analysis:

(*a*) A model case of punishment would be a boy who deliberately broke a window and was beaten for it by his headmaster. This would also be a model case of retribution.

(*b*) A contrary case of punishment would be if the boy were beaten without having done anything wrong. This is evidently not a case of retribution either. Why not? Because the treatment the boy receives is not retributive—he is not being *paid back* for anything he did, since he did nothing demanding retribution.

(*c*) As a related case we could consider whether his treatment was 'fair' or 'just'. Did he 'deserve' to be treated as he was in the two cases above? We would say 'Yes' to the first and 'No' to the second. The first treatment is 'fair' and 'just', the second might be called 'unfair' and 'unjust'.

(*d*) We could take as a borderline case a case in which someone has committed a crime but, instead of being hanged or going to prison, is sentenced by the judge to go to a mental asylum. This is odd or queer: is 'sentenced' really the right word? Perhaps he wants to go to the asylum: after all, 'asylum' normally means an escape, a refuge, somewhere nice to go. Would this be a 'punishment'? When we hesitate about what to call it, what exactly are we in doubt about? Is it perhaps whether going to the asylum is pleasant or unpleasant? Or is it because this treatment seems to have little connection with his crime? Surely this is not a case of retribution, anyway: the man has, let us say, committed a foul murder, and is not being paid back for it. We need a case which is more unlike what normally happens in British courts of justice than this case is.

(e) Thus we invent a case (perhaps absurd in practice) in which the man is given extremely pleasant treatment: suppose he is given a long holiday with pay, with attractive girls to look after him and free champagne. Now this certainly isn't punishment, nor retribution either: even if this treatment were ordered by a judge in an official court as the appropriate treatment for his crime, we still wouldn't want to call it punishment. The reason must be that it is in principle the wrong sort of treatment to count as punishment: it is pleasant and not nasty. This treatment too we would call 'unfair' or 'unjust': not so much in relation to this man in himself, but by comparison with the sort of treatment given to other criminals. This man has behaved badly and been rewarded: the other criminals behave badly and are punished. The whole situation is 'unfair': the rewards and punishments in this society are not properly dealt out. (Note that the concept of 'reward' goes closely with that of punishment.)

(*f*) Looking at the social context, we can see how the development of modern psychology (amongst other things) may suggest that we should revise our opinions on how to treat criminals in general. Hitherto, most societies, at most periods of history, have been content to treat criminals according to a simple law of retribution along the lines of 'An eye for an eye, and a tooth for a tooth'. But we may be worried about whether this is satisfactory: perhaps punishment should also reform the criminal—and certainly it ought to deter potential criminals. Hence the talk about 'reformative' and 'deterrent' punishment. The question 'Ought punishment to be retributive?' represents this social concern: we are worried about how we can fit in other objectives (the objectives of reforming the criminal and deterring potential criminals), or perhaps about whether we need to keep the notion of retribution at all. But then—going back to our use of techniques (*a*)–(*e*) as we used them above—it looks as if all cases of punishment are also, logically, cases of retribution. Can you logically have a non-retributive punishment? We must remember to pick up this point later.

(*g*) This might suggest one underlying anxiety on which the question is based. If punishment were never retributive—and perhaps this means never unpleasant—what would become of law and order? Surely we must do unpleasant things to criminals, otherwise there will be nothing to stop people committing crimes. This reintroduces the notion of punishment as a deterrent. Would it be possible to keep the deterrent factor without keeping the notion of retribution? We must revert to this point also.

(*h*) What would be the practical results of saying

'Yes' or 'No' to the question? If we say 'Yes', then we commit ourselves, it seems, to dealing out unpleasant treatment to anyone who commits a crime: for punishment, retribution, and unpleasant treatment seem to go logically together. But this only holds good as long as we insist on dealing out *punishment*. What would happen if we abandoned the word in the context of crime, and simply considered what sort of treatment (as opposed to what sort of punishment) we considered desirable? This would give us a freer hand in deciding on the treatment, for the concept of punishment seems to tie us down to one specific type of treatment, namely, unpleasant treatment. If we said 'No' to the question, it looks as if we might be contradicting ourselves: that is, if punishment logically implies retribution; and this would be a bad start to any social inquiry. It looks as if, for social purposes, we need first to get a clear grasp of what is *meant* by the words 'punishment' and 'retribution', and then ask some more neutral question like 'How should we treat criminals?'

(*i*) Whatever we make of the concepts of punishment and retribution, we do not want to muddle or confuse our language. It looks as if 'punishment' and the related words stand for quite distinct notions, and probably they are useful notions. We need only clarify the normal sense of these words, and are not called on to suggest new senses or interpretations. We seem to have established that punishment and retribution necessarily involve unpleasant treatment: perhaps they involve other things also, and we should investigate this further before wondering about whether the concepts need any drastic revision.

*Step III*

Now let us start our interior dialogue. First, let's pick up the points we made in the last step. Could we logically have a non-retributive punishment? And could we keep the deterrent factor without keeping the notion of retribution? Retribution seems to involve the idea of 'paying back': the boy who broke the window and the man who did the crime were paid back by somebody—the headmaster or the judge. This suggests that there has to be somebody who deliberately does the punishing, otherwise it doesn't count as punishment. Let's check this with a case. Suppose a criminal gets off scot-free so far as the law is concerned, but is beaten up by the relatives of his victim after his trial is over. Is this punishment? No, we would be more likely to describe it as *revenge*: it needs to be some properly con- stituted *authority* that punishes. Does it have to be a human agency? Suppose the same criminal gets run over by accident in the street: is this punishment? Surely not: we might say, in a religious mood (if we have that kind of religion) that 'God punished him', but this is a bit far-fetched. This shows that punishment isn't just a matter of someone getting unpleasant treat- ment, nor just a matter of getting unpleasant treatment *after* doing something bad, but of getting unpleasant treatment *for* doing something bad: and the word 'for' here represents deliberate action by a human agency entitled to take such action.

This begins to look more hopeful. 'Punishment' carries an unseen implication (page 41) with it: the implication of 'unpleasant treatment for, or in requital or retribution for, some bad action'. Let's now look back over the last step. The example in (*d*), where the criminal is sent to the asylum, may not be an example of punishment. If the judge is saying, in effect, 'We are not treating you as a criminal, but as a mental case, so we aren't trying to pay you back for the wrong you've done: however, we think it's best for you to go to an asylum', then the judge isn't punishing, he's just *treating* the man. Similarly in (*e*), the invented case, the criminal who gets a long holiday with pay isn't being punished, because his treatment isn't unpleasant. Of course we *could* call both these punishment if we insisted that anything which a judge decided to do about a criminal counted as punishment: but this would be stretching the meaning too far (page 43).

Thus it looks as if 'retributive punishment' says the same thing twice: punishment logically *must* be retributive. What about 'deterrent punishment' and 'reformative punishment'? Are these contradictory phrases? Not necessarily, because punishment *can* have deterrent and reformative effects, as well as satisfying the principle of retribution. However, there will be cases where the best treatment for deterring and/or reforming will not necessarily satisfy the principle of retribution: and in those cases, we cannot logically call the treatment 'punishment'. So, if ever we want to treat criminals in these ways, we shall have to drop the notion of punishment. Are we prepared to do this? Well, it depends whether we insist on keeping the notion of retribution. To some people it seems a good thing to exact retribution in all cases of wrong-doing: to others, this seems unnecessary. This is a matter of moral argument:

though it is not clear what useful objectives are served by insisting on retribution in all cases. Most of our objectives are adequately represented by the notions of deterrence and reform—these include our general concern with society and with the individual criminal.

However, perhaps this is beyond the scope of the question. The question 'Ought our treatment of criminals to be retributive?' is quite different. We might decide, in reference to this question, that the principle of retribution works quite well as a general rule, simply because it involves unpleasant treatment and such treatment has a good deterrent (and perhaps a good reformative) effect on people. But this is a question of sociological fact, to answer which we need statistics and not guess-work. It is possible that retributive treatment works well for some types of crimes but not others, or more precisely for some types of criminals but not others. All this may be worth saying, but we must not stray too far from the original question.

## Step IV

Taking another look at the question, we see that it now looks odd to ask '*Ought* punishment to be retributive?' Logically it *must* be. What we have to do, therefore, in order to make our answer as effective as possible, is to prove this logical point first, and then to sketch other possible lines of approach to deal with the questions which may underlie this question: questions like 'Ought our *treatment* of criminals to be retributive?' or 'Ought punishment to be *only* retributive?' We need not go far along these lines, since these were not the questions which we were asked to answer: but it would be interesting to make some attempt.

## Step V

We now look for the quickest and most convincing way of proving the logical points—and first, the point that punishment logically entails retribution. We could list our points as follows:

(a) 'Retribution', in ordinary English, means 'paying back'; it is similar to 'requital'. We talk of 'exacting retribution', using a metaphor apparently derived from paying debts. Hence 'an eye for an eye and a tooth for a tooth'.

(b) What counts as punishment? Here we take the cases in the interior dialogue in the last step: the cases of the criminal who gets pleasant treatment, and the criminal who gets run over by a bus. Neither of these would be called 'punishment' in normal usage. This can only be because essential criteria for the concept are missing. These criteria are (i) unpleasant treatment, and (ii) unpleasant treatment *for*, or in retribution for, a bad action, (iii) such unpleasant treatment must be carried out by someone *entitled* to do so. We could amplify and illustrate this from other examples which we used when applying the techniques in step II; say, the boy breaking a window, or the criminal being sent to an asylum. Since all this is so, punishment logically entails retribution.

(c) Therefore the question '*Ought* punishment to be retributive?' is logically odd: because, in English, punishment *is* retributive. Could we rephrase it to read 'Ought our treatment of criminals to be retributive?'

or 'Ought punishment to be only retributive?' Is this what the questioner is worried about? If so, then we can put forward some ideas.

(d) Taking 'Ought punishment to be only retributive?', we might reasonably call this a silly question. Anyone would wish punishment, if possible, to deter potential criminals, reform actual criminals, or benefit society in any other possible way. Obviously the answer is 'No': punishment can and should have other uses.

(e) Taking 'Ought our treatment of criminals to be retributive?', we might say

(i) No apparent point is served by retribution, solely for its own sake.

(ii) It is more than likely that the desire for retribution is irrational, and whilst satisfying urges in society and in the individual's mind leads to no particularly desirable results.

(iii) On the other hand, retribution may be quite good as a working principle in society, and as a working principle it may be justified because it achieves desirable objectives such as deterrence and reform: but this is a question of sociological fact, to answer which we need a good deal more research.

(f) Whatever the fundamental worry of the questioner, it would be best to ask a more neutral question such as 'How should we treat our criminals?', and hence avoid the logical implications of words like 'punishment' and 'retribution'. To discuss the matter while retaining the word 'punishment' is to beg the question, since punishment is necessarily retributive.

(g) We might interpret the question (page 37) to mean 'Is it useful and desirable in language to tie down

the word "punishment" to the word "retribution"?'
This is an odd question: in fact 'punishment' *is* tied to
'retribution', and tied very tightly too. If we untied it,
we should only have to invent another word to mean
'unpleasant treatment dealt out (by one entitled to do
so) for a bad action', and this seems rather a waste of
time. Our language works perfectly well in this area,
provided we remain conscious of the meanings of the
words involved.

All this might appear as brief notes in the following
form:

   (i) Meaning of 'retribution' (from ordinary
English usage).

   (ii) Meaning of 'punishment' (three criteria:
cases to illustrate these).

   (iii) Hence punishment entails retribution: therefore the question logically odd.

   (iv) Re-interpretations of the question: (1) '...only
retributive?'—silly question. (2) '...treatment of
criminals...?' Purpose of retribution? Motives for
it? Useful as a working principle? A factual question
needing more research. (3) Need for a neutral question,
not involving concepts like punishment, if we are
worried about society. (4) Demand to alter the meaning
of everyday words? Pointless.

## Step VI

We must now try and cast this in the form of a brief
essay. Naturally one could write at almost any length
on the question: for the purposes of practical illustration
I shall assume a time period of about forty minutes to
include both the previous steps and the actual writing.

How much time you spend, out of this forty minutes, on the preliminary steps and how much on the writing is partly a matter of taste: but, as I mentioned earlier, it is best to cover the preliminary ground thoroughly first and not to start writing until you know almost exactly what you are going to say. This means that your actual writing time should not amount to much more than twenty minutes: though if the preliminary work is easy you might get through it more quickly, and extend the writing time to thirty minutes. However, this is essentially a matter of practice and of trial and error: and different rules suit different people.

*Essay: 'Ought punishment to be retributive?'* Before making a value-judgement that *A* ought to be *B*, we must first be sure that we are fully conscious of the meaning and use of both *A* and *B*. With the concept of retribution there is little difficulty. 'Retribution' means 'repayment' or 'requital'. We talk of 'exacting retribution', just as we talk of exacting payment for a debt. A criminal who steals or murders is regarded as having incurred a debt: society exacts repayment or retribution from him by making him spend time in prison or by executing him. Though there may be practical problems about how much retribution or what kind of retribution (if any) to exact, there are no serious logical problems about the nature of the concept.

The notion of punishment, however, is more complex; and it can be seen that three conditions must exist if treatment is to count as punishment. First, the treatment must be unpleasant. If a criminal committed a foul and deliberate murder and was 'sentenced' to a long holiday with pay, we would not describe this as punishment—even if it were ordered by a properly constituted legal authority. Secondly, the unpleasant treatment must be deliberately dealt out by a person *for* or *in respect of* the criminal's wrongdoing. Thus if a criminal were acquitted by a court, but were shortly afterwards run over by a bus or struck by lightning, we would not call this punishment—except, perhaps, in virtue of some metaphysical belief whereby we might want to say 'God punished him'. Thirdly, it must be dealt out by a properly constituted authority. We may take one more case, in which a criminal is found technically guilty of his crime, but is sent to a mental asylum instead of prison. Is this punishment? We would probably say not, because we would be uncertain about whether either of the first two criteria mentioned above were applicable. It is not clear (i) that going to a mental asylum (for this particular man) is unpleasant, nor (ii) that this is really a *sentence* dealt out to him *for* his crime.

These criteria—and particularly the second—seem to show that the notion of retribution is integral to the concept of punishment: more briefly, punishment necessarily and logically implies retribution—otherwise it would not be punishment but some other kind of treatment. Hence the question is logically curious: there seems little point in asking whether punishment ought to be retributive when logically it must be. However, the question may be a clumsy way of expressing other questions which it would be more profitable to ask. Thus one could rephrase it to read 'Ought punishment to be *only* retributive?', or perhaps (more drastically but more usefully) 'Ought our treatment of criminals to be retributive?'

The first of these rephrased questions leads nowhere: for few people would not wish punishment to satisfy other conditions as well as the condition of exacting retribution. One would wish a punishment to deter potential criminals, to reform the actual criminal, and in general to exercise a beneficial or curative effect on society. The second question, however, opens up a very wide field. First, it is not at all clear what beneficial results are achieved by retribution as an end in itself: it may be held as a moral principle that the wicked should be made to suffer, but it is hard to see how it could be defended. Secondly, a desire for exacting retribution seems psychologically and ethically suspect, and is hardly consistent with the creeds and outlooks preached (though rarely practised) by most modern civilisations. It may be possible to defend retribution as a working principle in society, on the grounds that retributive treatment does in fact and in practice satisfy other ends—for instance, the objectives of deterring and reforming. But this is a question of sociological fact: and to answer it properly we need statistics rather than guess-work.

If we are socially concerned with treatment of criminals or rule-breakers in general, it would be wiser to ask a question which does not involve us in complex concepts: some such simple question as 'How should we treat criminals?' To use the word 'punishment' pre-judges the issue: for 'punishment', as we saw, specifies a certain type of treatment. It would, theoretically, be possible to alter the meaning of 'punishment', so as to untie it from the notion of retribution: we should perhaps then have made it synonymous with 'treatment'. But there seems little point in attempting such linguistic revision. Once we are conscious of the implications of the word 'punishment', it is probable that we shall prefer to discuss our social problems in other and less highly charged language.

### Step VII

We now look back over this essay, and have left ourselves a little time for corrections. We notice the following:

(a) We started off the first paragraph with the phrase 'Before making a value-judgement', but never actually fulfilled the implication that we were going to make such a judgement. Something must be said about this. The best place is the third paragraph. Instead of saying 'there seems little point in asking whether punishment ought to be retributive when logically it must be', let us say 'it is not clear what could be meant by asking whether punishment *ought* to be retributive, when logically it *must* be: and hence we cannot, as we at first implied, make any sensible judgement of value about it'.

(b) In the second paragraph the third sentence gives a reason for the second: that is, our example is supposed to prove the criterion of unpleasantness. To make this absolutely clear, it might be better to start the third sentence '*For* if a criminal...'.

(c) In the middle of the second paragraph, where we are talking about the idea of 'God punished him', have we really expressed this idea clearly? Are we really clear about it ourselves? It looks as if we either ought to expand this point, or else cut it out. Perhaps we ought simply to write '...we would not normally call this punishment in any straightforward sense', and end the sentence there.

(d) In the fourth paragraph, first sentence: 'few people would not wish' is unnecessarily complicated. Rewrite it as 'nearly everybody would wish'.

(e) In the middle of the fourth paragraph we say 'it may be held as a moral principle that the wicked should be made to suffer, but it is hard to see how it could be defended'. Do we really mean this? Actually various defences could be made, including the one mentioned later in the paragraph, the defence that it is a good working principle. We had better add something like '...defended as an end in itself' or '...defended as a desirable thing in itself'.

(f) At the end of the fourth paragraph, where we say 'But this is a question of sociological fact...' we have been far too brusque. We need to say something like 'But this view, if it is to be adequately assessed, needs far greater sociological knowledge than we possess at present: it may seem plausible, but there is little point in indulging in guess-work in the present context'.

(g) At the beginning of the fifth paragraph, we call the question 'How should we treat criminals?' a *simple* question. This it certainly is not, in at least one obvious sense. We should either delete the word, or explain somehow that we mean logically simple, free from difficult concepts and emotionally charged words.

In going through the steps in this procedure I have tried to move as slowly as could reasonably be expected. The reader will feel—and I think ought to feel—that many points could have been dispensed with: also that some points should have been expanded, and perhaps other points introduced. Obviously, for instance, a good deal more could be written to fill out the last part of the essay, on the rephrased questions, since this opens up the whole field of criminal reform and many other fields as well: but I do not think this is strictly within the terms of reference set by the question, although it adds some points of interest and takes the whole matter a little further than the brief and rather dry proof of the fact that 'punishment' is logically tied to 'retribution'. It is more arguable that we should have spent more time proving this, and noting other logically interesting things about the concept, and less time trying to answer sociological questions which we were not strictly asked. However, as long as we realise that we *must* do justice to the original question, whatever other ground we want to cover, we can safely say that this is a matter of opinion—perhaps even a matter of taste.

## B. '*Is astrology a science?*'

*Step I*

We notice (page 23) that this is a mixed question, involving both knowledge of the nature of astrology and an understanding of the concept of science, and decide therefore to deal with the question of concept first.

*Step II*

(*a*) A model case of a science would perhaps be astronomy, though obviously there are plenty of others. We might gain some advantage from taking astronomy, since it has something in common with astrology (both have to do with stars and planets).

(*b*) A contrary case might also be invented, which has to do with stars. Suppose somebody painted an impressionistic picture of the stars, or wrote a poem about them. These activities are certainly not sciences: we should call them arts. In a sense their subject-matter is the same: like astronomy, they have to do with the stars. But they approach it from a different angle, or with a different purpose.

(*c*) What concepts are related to science? Perhaps the notion of knowledge: but this isn't very closely related, because there are all sorts of knowledge that aren't scientific. You can know Latin, mathematics, how to swim, who the Prime Minister was in 1888, and so on. What about knowledge of nature? This is a bit closer, but not close enough: one could plausibly say that someone like Wordsworth or Constable, or perhaps farmers and peasants, 'knew nature'. But they don't know *about* nature in the same way that scientists do. They have factual knowledge, but they aren't able to frame laws and hypotheses, and they don't make experiments. Perhaps these are some of the criteria for science.

(*d*) What other things are on the borderline of science, besides astrology? Suppose we take psychology. Now psychologists do know some things about human beings: they do frame laws and hypotheses: they do make experiments. But we're still not sure that psychology is a science. Why not? Perhaps we feel that they don't tell us the truth always: but then, neither do physicists or astronomers—every branch of science has made mistakes. Isn't it rather that we sometimes feel they don't tell us anything that we don't already know? Perhaps we feel that what they say is either nonsense or obvious. Let's try another borderline case—meteorology, or the predicting of weather. Is this a science? It seems to depend on whether the meteorologists can really predict better than the ordinary person: whether all their experiments and hypotheses are really worth anything. So perhaps prediction is the most important criterion.[1] But perhaps the experiments and hypotheses are also important.

(e) So let's invent a case where you get admirable predictions but no scientific paraphernalia. Suppose I look in a crystal ball and predict the winner of the Derby accurately every year: assume I have no idea how I do it, and conduct no experiments or anything— I just look, and then tell you the winner. Is this a science? Certainly not. Why not? Perhaps it's because I don't have any equipment except my crystal ball, and

---

[1] I do not think that we can count predictive ability as an *essential* criterion. Botany and anatomy, for instance, are normally counted as sciences: but their main work and function consists in classification rather than prediction. But predictive ability is very important: even the work of classification tends to result in greater powers of prediction, because the things classified are grouped together because of important characteristics which they have in common, and the greater awareness of these characteristics improves our ability to predict how the things will behave in the future. Indeed there would be no point or purpose— at any rate, no scientific purpose—in classifying things in this way unless it assisted our understanding of the way they worked, and hence (inevitably) improved our predictive powers.

don't do experiments. But now, suppose I bought a vast mass of equipment and surrounded my crystal ball with wires and tubes, and every now and then poured different-coloured liquids into test-tubes, and so on, would this help? No, it wouldn't: we should say that I had dressed the thing up to *look like* a science, but it wasn't really. For one thing, I hadn't arrived at my predictions by a process of reasoning and observation: the equipment and pseudo-experiments weren't really *connected* with my predictions. So now it looks as if we have some more criteria: (i) the activity has to tell us more than we know already; (ii) it has to do this, not by guesswork, divine inspiration or whatever, but by observation, experiment, the testing of hypotheses by experiment, and so on. Science is not just knowledge: it is knowledge the average man could not produce for himself, and knowledge organised in a particular and complex way so as to produce results.

(*f*) This question might crop up in a social context if, say, we were wondering whether to teach astrology at school or at a university. 'Is it a science?' would mean 'Is it worth teaching?' We know science is worth teaching, for one good reason at least—because it is useful. With science we can improve our standard of living, defend ourselves against attack, send men into space, and so on. Will astrology produce any useful results? Obviously this depends on whether it produces knowledge that we could not otherwise obtain, as mentioned in (*e*) above.

(*g*) Is there any underlying anxiety here? Are we perhaps worried that astrology *may* be a science without our knowing it—that we may be dismissing it too easily? But then all we have to do is to test whether it produces genuine and otherwise unobtainable knowledge. Or are we worried in the opposite way—that we may be tempted, just because it ends in 'ology', to admit it as a science, whereas we want to keep the qualifications for counting as a 'science' as high as possible: we want to guard the concept jealously, and not run the risk of contaminating 'true' sciences with pseudo-sciences. But then this too depends simply on whether astrology passes the relevant tests for 'science': on whether it satisfies the criteria.

(h) The practical results of saying 'Yes' or 'No' to this question are fairly obvious. If we count astrology as a science, then we might expect textbooks to be written about it, and have it taught in educational institutions. There would be professors of astrology, and astrological members of the Royal Society. Here we see the practical sharpness of the question: what we are concerned with is whether astrology is really mumbo-jumbo or perfectly respectable. If it is mumbo-jumbo, or even if it has nothing important to offer, then we do not want to waste our money on it. But this too depends on whether it can offer genuine knowledge.

(i) If we find that astrology satisfies some of the criteria but not others, we might want to call it a science, even if this means stretching the concept a little beyond its normal limits. We should only do this if, on consideration, we found that it satisfied—or perhaps could in principle satisfy—the most important criteria. (Thus we could say, though dangerously, that psychology ought to count as a science, because it could in principle satisfy all the criteria even if it does not at present do so.) On the other hand, if it satisfies none of the criteria, or only the less important ones, we have no reason to extend the concept of science to include it.

## Step III. The interior dialogue

Let's first have another look at the criteria for science, since our ideas on this point are still rather hazy. First, it must, typically, have some powers of prediction beyond the capabilities of the average man. Anybody can predict rain if a storm-cloud is coming his way: but for meteorology to be a science it must predict rain when the average man can't. (But supposing it *occasionally* predicted successfully when the average man couldn't? This isn't quite good enough: at least we'd have to be sure that it wasn't just luck. So we need reasonably *consistent* predictions which are successful.)

Secondly, the prediction must issue as the result of some organised technique. Does there have to be complex equipment? Not really: you could do astronomy with fair success just by using your eyes and thinking. But then, isn't that just what the crystal-gazer in (*e*) above does? Not quite, because he doesn't observe anything and then put two and two together, and then check up on his theories, in the way that somebody who watched the movements of the planets and then evolved some theory about them would do. So there has to be some sort of technique, observation, reasoning, experiment, and so forth. It isn't just that the scientist can predict: it's also that his prediction is firmly based on his observations and theories. This is how he can *explain* why, say, an eclipse will occur, or why the litmus paper will turn red.

Is the notion of *explanation* a necessary criterion? Let's invent a case where all the other criteria are satisfied but not this one. Take the example of elementary astronomy used earlier. We observe (by means of telescopes and other complex equipment) stars and planets, and we notice that they move in certain regular orbits over certain time periods. By dint of constant observation, but *no theorising about causes*, we reach a position in which we can predict accurately what planets will be in what part of the sky at certain times. This is something that the average man could not work out for himself: but is it science? We might think also of someone who spent a lot of time watching the behaviour of birds in his garden, so that he could predict things about them which the ordinary person could not predict: is this science? We might prefer to say that it was the making of observations *preliminary* to science. But these are obviously borderline cases: and, in fact, we were misleading when we said that *no* element of explanation and *no* 'theorising about causes' took place. For the star-watcher would say things like 'Venus will appear on the horizon in an hour's time, *because* it always does at this time of the year, provided that so-and-so isn't the case...', and the bird-watcher could say things like 'Well, that blue-tit will enter the hole in the coconut, *because* when there's snow on the ground blue-tits always do, unless there are insects about which they can eat...', and so on. This is, perhaps, different in kind from 'proper' science where the reasons are not *simply* in terms of what has happened in the past: but it is not radically different, and we can't use the criterion of explanation or theorising to make a sharp dividing line between science and intelligent observation.

Now what about astrology? This is a factual rather than a conceptual matter. We know that astrologers do commit themselves (or appear to commit themselves) to predictions based on an alleged connection between the positions of the stars and human life. People born under a certain sign of the Zodiac are supposed to be of a certain temperament: when planet $A$ is in conjunction with planet $B$, this is supposed to mean that the time is favourable for love, or war, or business deals, and so on. Certainly astrology makes claims as if it were a science: it claims to predict where the ordinary man cannot, by the use of skilled techniques (expert knowledge of what the movements of stars mean, the casting of horoscopes, etc.), with reasonably consistent success.

Does astrology make good these claims? We don't know, because it isn't clear that a proper test has been imposed upon it. You would have to have several controlled experiments, in which groups of astrologers and groups of ordinary people, each in possession of the same facts and the same general intellectual ability (except that the astrologers would have their 'expert knowledge'), were asked to predict. The predictions would have to be definite and verifiable, otherwise there is no way of testing their accuracy. (A prediction like 'If you have any money today, you will probably spend some' is not very helpful.) For astrology to come out as a science the astrologers would need to show (i) that they consistently and successfully predicted more than the ordinary people, and (ii) that they did this *in virtue of* their 'expert knowledge', and not just by clairvoyance. Even then we might think that it was only a science in the same (loose) sense that the star-watcher and the bird-watcher in the examples above were doing science: that is, the astrologers might have to say 'Well, we don't know why, but it just happens that when Mars is in the ascendant and in conjunction with Venus, then this is a good time for army officers to get married'. In other words, the amount of explanation and theorising about causes may be insufficient for it to count as a science: it may be simply in the preliminary stage of general observation.

A final thought: things don't count as sciences unless they have been shown to be properly scientific. If astrology had been a science, the chances are that it would have proved itself before now (though not necessarily: consider extra-sensory perception, the study of which is perhaps just beginning to be a science). One would certainly not wish it taught at school and at the university in the faint hope that, when we get down to running these tests on it, it may turn out to be a science. We can certainly say 'There may be something in it': but to say this is not to say very much. There may be something in crystal-gazing, witchcraft, spiritualism, alchemy, clairvoyance, and telling fortunes by cards: but this gives not the slightest reason why we should for a moment consider them even as potential sciences. They may be mumbo-jumbo. Rational people do not believe things unless there is some good evidence for them.

*Step IV*

Taking another look at the question, we see that it presents no new difficulty: we are asked simply to say whether astrology fits into the concept of science. We might rephrase this, if we feel like it, as 'Would it be sensible to count astrology as a science?', but not much is gained by this, except the overt acknowledgement that the question is a conceptual one.

*Step V*

We must now try to get down as concisely as possible the various logical points we have made, in a coherent order:

(*a*) The concept of science is distinguished from mumbo-jumbo on the one hand and from ordinary knowledge possessed by the average man on the other.

(*b*) A science is a corpus of factual knowledge and theory about the phenomena of nature, and is logically unlike art, guess-work, aesthetic appreciation, etc.

(*c*) The criteria for a science seem to be:

(i) the ability to predict with reasonably consistent success in areas where the ordinary man cannot do so;

(ii) the predictions must be firmly based on a body of observation, theory, and perhaps also on the use of experiment and complex equipment, in such a way that they can be seen to *issue from* this.

Perhaps we could put these two points by saying that science is a *sophisticated* body of knowledge, or a *highly organised* method of obtaining knowledge.

(*d*) Though successful prediction as in (i) above is perhaps the most important criterion, the necessity of explanation and theorising as in (ii) represents a looser criterion. We might draw a distinction between the preliminary stages of science (or perhaps before science), and 'proper' science: the cases of amateur astronomy and bird-watching are relevant here.

(e) Astrology claims, at least, to satisfy these criteria, on an alleged connection between stars and human life.

(f) These claims have not been proved. To prove them, we should need certain tests and experiments, carefully designed to make sure that both criteria were satisfied.

(g) It seems unlikely that astrology could satisfy them, since it has not done so. Thus it would not be sensible, either from a logical or a sociological point of view, to count it as a science.

This might appear in note form as follows:

(i)  Science is unlike (1) mumbo-jumbo; (2) art, aesthetic appreciation, etc; and (3) ordinary amateur knowledge.

(ii)  Science is a corpus of fact and theory about nature.

(iii)  Criteria: (1) consistent and successful prediction, (2) this prediction as issuing from its observations, theories, etc., at least to some extent.

(iv)  Distinction between 'proper' science and the preliminary stage of observation.

(v)  Astrology claims to satisfy these criteria, but this not proved. Tests needed.

(vi)  Until the tests are passed, unwise to count astrology as a science.

*Step VI. The complete essay*

What is a science? We know that astronomy, physics, chemistry and so on are sciences: whereas poetry, painting, swimming, etc., are not. We see from this that, at least, a science must be concerned with learning and stating facts about the natural world (as opposed to creating works of art, learning skills, and so forth). But this cannot be a sufficient condition for science: alchemy and fortune-telling, on the one hand, and the everyday knowledge of the natural world possessed by the ordinary layman on the other, do not qualify as sciences, even though both seem concerned to learn and state facts. The criteria of science are more stringent.

The first criterion is that the activity should enable one to predict, with reasonably consistent success, in a way in which the ordinary man with ordinary knowledge cannot predict. Thus the ordinary man may be able to predict that there will be rain if he sees a storm-cloud coming his way: but only an expert meteorologist could predict rain in the absence of such obvious signs. The whole body of observations, hypotheses, experiments, laws, theories, and the complex and sophisticated equipment of what we call a 'science', shows a degree of organisation of knowledge much higher than that possessed by common sense: and it is in virtue of this that such sophisticated predictions as the prediction of an eclipse or an atomic reaction are possible.

However, this criterion is not essential. It is also insufficient. We could imagine a person who was clairvoyant, or had consistently reliable 'hunches', making consistently accurate predictions: but this would not count as science. The mere *possession* of complex equipment and a sophisticated technique is inadequate to rectify this defect: for a fortune-teller, for instance, might use crystal balls, a complex system of laying out cards and interpreting them, and so forth, and also make accurate predictions, and still not qualify as a scientist. The sophisticated technique must be seen to be the base from which the predictions issue: the two must be rationally connected. Our second criterion, then, is that if a science is concerned with predictions, these must be derived from a highly organised corpus of observation, experiment, theory, etc.

This second criterion is rather loose, and we can imagine cases in which predictions could be made with striking success, but in which the theoretical basis of those predictions was so insubstantial that we would hesitate before calling these cases of science. Thus anyone who spends a lot of time watching the stars, or observing the behaviour of birds, can predict more successfully than the average man—just as a cook can predict the behaviour of certain solids and liquids better than someone who does no cooking. Nor, in these cases, is there any mumbo-jumbo, as with the fortune-teller. But we might think there to be insufficient theory and insufficient explanation or investigation of causes behind such predictions: the activity is not highly organised or sophisticated enough to count as science.

Astrology certainly claims to be a science: that is, it is not an art, a skill, or just good fun. The claim is that events in human life can be predicted by considering the stars and planets. Unfortunately astrology so far has not been proved to meet either criterion: we do not know, either that astrologers can in fact predict with consistent accuracy and greater success than the average man, or that these predictions (if they are successful) issue from the 'technique' of astrology. We should have to conduct stringent tests, pitting control groups of astrologers against other groups of non-astrologers, and also investigate the connection between astrological predictions and astrological theory, in order to prove any sort of case for astrology: and it seems unlikely, in view of the extreme age of this pseudo-science, that the case would be proved, since there has been plenty of time for astrologers to prove it. There may, of course, be 'something in it' which may eventually be worth scientific study, as is now the case with the phenomena of extra-sensory perception. But at present there seems no point in extending the limits of the concept of science so as to include astrology.

### Step VII. Corrections

(a) In the third paragraph the point is not very clearly made. Before the last sentence of the paragraph, after 'rationally connected', we should say something like 'The successful fortune-teller does not know *why* his guesses are accurate, nor does his equipment help him in this respect'.

(b) In the same paragraph, 'the base from which the predictions issue' is poor English: say 'the base on which the predictions are founded', or something similar.

(c) In the fourth paragraph the point about the looseness of the criterion is not immediately and directly made. Make the first sentence read: 'This second criterion is rather loose. How highly organised does this corpus of observation, etc., have to be? We can imagine cases....'

(d) In the fifth paragraph the implication of the first

sentence is that by mentioning 'an art, a skill, or just good fun' we have exhausted the possibilities of all non-scientific activities. But the case of mathematics, for instance, shows that this isn't so. We must say 'a recognisably separate academic discipline, an art, a skill, just good fun, or anything else of the kind'. This is not a very good emendation, but it will do.

(e) In the second sentence of the fifth paragraph this is supposed to be a claim to be a science, and as such it is not full enough. We should rather say 'The claim is that events in human life can be predicted with consistent and remarkable success by a skilled and expert consideration of the stars and planets'.

(f) At the end of the fifth paragraph have we really made the point about there perhaps being 'something in it'? If we have time, it would be better to make a new paragraph after '...for astrologers to prove it', beginning: 'This is not necessarily to dismiss astrology as pure mumbo-jumbo. There may be something in it...' and perhaps fill out the rest more fully.

CHAPTER III

# PHILOSOPHY AND ANALYSIS

Although this is primarily a textbook written for a specific purpose, I said in the Preface that it ought to be useful to ordinary people in the ordinary course of their lives—that is, not just to those who face a general paper, or have to do a course in philosophy. This is not just a pious hope: but it may seem rather a forlorn one, because the gap between philosophy and ordinary life is horrifyingly large. Consequently it may be useful to say something about the way in which the techniques illustrated in this book come into philosophy, and the way in which philosophy may come into ordinary life. Of course this is an immense subject, and I cannot do it justice: but I hope at least to show that the ordinary person may justifiably be more optimistic about the relevance of philosophy than perhaps some philosophers have led him to expect.

Everything turns on the business of philosophy. One view, perhaps still the most popular, is that philosophy is directly and immediately concerned with a way of life and with the truth about reality. It has to do with what people are, what they do, and what they feel: with their behaviour, their emotions, their beliefs and moral judgements. By this account a man's philosophy is a sort of blend between his motives, his behaviour, and his values. Thus one may pursue pleasure, think pleasure good, and be labelled a hedonist or a utilitarian: another may listen to the dictates of conscience, act from a sense of duty, and be labelled a Kantian or an intuitionist. These are their philosophies. Philosophy as a whole makes a living, on this theory, by outlining various philosophies and attempting to judge between them. Plato will paint you one kind of life, Aristotle another, Bertrand Russell a third: different philosophers will criticise different ways of life, and the individual reads them and then chooses for himself. This is still perhaps the most common view of philosophy. Some people declare themselves 'on the side of logic', others 'on the side of the emotions': some believe in duty, others in happiness: some in mysticism, others in hard fact.

The objection to this picture is that it makes of the philosopher no more than the manager of an art gallery in which paintings of different ways of life are displayed, held up to the light, criticised, valued, and finally bought. The philosopher exhibits these, explains them, assesses them, and so forth. People buy what suits them. There appears to be no real place for *rational* assessment, no criteria by which one painting may be firmly judged better than another. Various alternative choices are offered: you can buy an Epicurus or one of the Stoic school of painting, a Bentham or a Kant, a D. H. Lawrence or an Archbishop of Canterbury. Debate over which to buy becomes desultory and purposeless. All this may be amusing, and may improve mutual tolerance: but it signally fails to satisfy the intense demand for truth, the need to know as exactly as possible what is so and what is not so, and the desire for some effective tool or method by which to judge, all of which are as common in the twentieth century as they ever were.

The second view, which is still practised if not preached by the modern linguistic philosophers of Oxbridge, is a sharp and radical reaction from the first. On this view the philosopher has no *direct* connection with ways of life, motives, behaviour or values at all. He is an analyst of language, concerned with the verification and meaning of statements and with the logical use of words. The philosopher is not interested in what people think about life (much less how they choose to behave), but only in the words in which they express their thoughts. Do statements about God have meaning? Is the notion of truth applicable to moral judgements? What is meant by saying that a man acts freely? These are linguistic questions, which turn on the use of words like 'meaning', 'truth', 'freely', and so forth.

Plainly such radicalism has a lot to be said for it. For some thousands of years men have been discussing God, right and wrong, truth and falsehood, beauty, intuition, freedom and so on: and it is both plausible and probably true to say that in an important sense they did not know what they were talking about, in that none of the concepts which they used in their philosophies were ever properly subjected to analytic scrutiny. Plainly there is little point in discussing what is right and wrong unless we know what is meant by the words 'right' and 'wrong': and so with all questions. Moreover, it is a dangerous illusion to suppose that we do, in all senses, know the meanings of words. We may use them correctly, but we are not fully conscious of how they function logically in language: and to be unconscious of this may lead us into asking mistaken or even meaningless questions.

But as a complete programme for philosophy this will not do. It will not do primarily because language is not an abstract activity, but a form of life. It is something used by people; and not only this, but something much more close to people, much more *a part of them*, than most linguistic philosophers suppose. A man's language is *only a symptom* of his conceptual equipment, just as his neurotic behaviour-patterns are only symptoms of his inner psychic state. The phrase 'conceptual equipment' covers far more ground than language: though the analysis of language is one way—and a good way—of investigating conceptual equipment. To discover the stance in which a man faces the world, and to make him conscious of it so that he can change it, one good method is to see how he talks and make him conscious of his language.

Yet words represent only one part of the equipment with which people face life. When we say, for instance, 'He sees life differently from the way I see it', we do not mean *either* (as the first view claims) that he has a different way of life from me, that his behaviour-patterns, motives and values are different, *or* (according to the second view) just that he makes different sorts of statements from the ones I make, that he uses language differently. Of course both these may be true, and probably will be true: yet this is not what we mean when we say 'He sees life differently'. We mean that his conceptual equipment is different. It is as if we said, as we frequently do,

'He speaks a different language', using this sentence metaphorically, or 'It's no good, we don't speak the same language'. Here we are, significantly and interestingly, extending the notion of language to cover far more than the spoken symbols of words: we refer to the whole pattern of thought, the categories, concepts and modes of thinking, which lie behind both the man's way of life and his actual, spoken words.

Of all the beings we know, man alone is capable of entertaining the notion of meaning. This is to say that man has experiences in a different sense from that in which we might say, if we wished, that animals or inanimate objects have experiences. Dogs are beaten, roses suffer blight, lakes are drained and mountains levelled: but these occurrences do not *mean* anything to their victims; they simply *happen* to them. The victims act and are acted upon: they 'have experiences' in this sense, but in this sense only. With men, however, to have the power of saying 'I had a ghastly experience yesterday' is itself to have the power of conscious experience: of being conscious of what happens to one and what one does, of remembering it, naming and describing it, thinking about it and interpreting it. Man has the freedom to attach, within limits circumscribed by his own nature, whatever force or weight to his experiences he likes: the freedom to give them meaning.

If we give the concept of meaning or interpretation a wide sense, we see that it enters into all activities or occurrences of which we are at any time conscious. We are most inclined, as philosophers, to lay stress on those

cases where we are fully conscious of giving and understanding meaning: as for instance in the artificially
created symbols of mathematics, or to a lesser extent in
words. But whether we choose to lie in the sun, to
watch a blue and sparkling sea, to make love, to read a
novel, to order a particular wine, to buy a particular
car or even to smoke one more cigarette, our choices
are very obviously governed by the weight or force
which these happenings have for our minds: and this is
to say, in a sense, that they are governed by our own
interpretation or evaluation of them. The sun, the sea,
the lovemaking, and so on, all mean something to us:
and conflicts arise, pre-eminently in personal relationships, because different things mean differently to
different people.

Many of our interpretations are, no doubt, in some
sense forced upon us. We grow up into a world in
which, for the sake of survival, we are forced to attach
a certain weight to food, warmth, physical objects, and
so on: and thereby we uncritically create and accept a
framework of interpretation which, for the most part,
stays with us for the rest of our lives. Events happen
to us in early childhood which unconsciously exercise
power over the conscious activities of our later lives, by
forcing upon us certain interpretations and evaluations.
Some of these may be acceptable and beneficial, like the
desire for food: others may be unacceptable and tiresome, like a fear of cats or running water. Later we
acquire, more or less consciously, a framework of
attitudes and values towards all the aspects of human
life that we meet: to men, women, children and all the
roles that these may play (fathers, sisters, lovers, etc.),

to money and possessions, to nature, to our own role in society, to music and literature and the arts, to science, mathematics, philosophy and all the other disciplines of mankind. This framework is our conceptual equipment.

To describe conceptual equipment, to expand the meaning of the phrase, is not easy. One can use many metaphors, each as good or as bad as any other, to give a general idea of what we are talking about. At any particular period of his life, each man faces himself and the world by adopting a certain posture, a certain stance, towards it. Thus he may cower, stand erect, thrust his chin and his fists forward, wait passively for fate to overtake him, and so on. Or else we shall say that he faces things with a certain set of tools: the incisive, straightforward tool-kit of the physicist, the less informative but deeper probes and sounders of psychoanalysis, etc. Or else we shall say that he sees through different sets of spectacles: rose-tinted spectacles, or the dark glasses of pessimism, or the tough, protective goggles of the skier or motor racer. Or else we shall say that he speaks certain languages and understands them: the language of strict and authoritarian morality, or the kinder but more uncertain language of the liberal, the clear-cut vocabulary of the natural scientist or the emotively charged and symbolic language of the poet or the religious believer. Or else we say, finally, that he has the skill to play a certain number of games in life: the game of working with his colleagues, the game of taking part in dramatic or musical productions, the game of love.

Of these metaphors perhaps the most productive is

that of a game. Almost all human behaviour, and all
behaviour which has any claim to be in any sense
rational, is artificial. Consciously or unconsciously,
people obey or try to obey certain rules. These may be
rules of procedure, as in a law-court: rules of conven-
tion, as in personal relationships at a casual level: rules
of reasoning, as in logic or the study of some specific
subject: rules of behaviour in their moral lives: rules of
language in ordinary communication, and so forth.
More subtly, but still within the analogy, they follow
certain principles in their deeper personal relationships
and their approach to the arts. Learning to get on with
people, and (less obviously but still truly) learning to
love someone or to be a close friend of someone, is like
learning to play a game, just as learning to practise law
or to play the piano is like learning to play a game. We
can describe, and fruitfully, people who fail in one way
or another as failing because of *lack of skill*. People who
do not enjoy music (unless they are tone-deaf) fail to
enjoy it because they approach it in the wrong way:
they have not the skill to listen properly. Juvenile
delinquents simply do not know how to play a life-game
in which the criminal and civil law of the land forms
part of the rules. New nations, trying democracy for the
first time, often fail because they lack the feel of democratic procedure: there are certain tacit assumptions
which must be observed if parliamentary debates are
not to break down, and these are like rules in a game
which some players do not understand. A final example
from a field which is more obviously connected with our
present conception of philosophy: people who reject
religion *in toto* often do so because, as it were, they can-

not find their way around the conceptual landscape of religion. The concepts and experiences of religion (like those of poetry or music) form a game which it takes skill, practice and study to play.

To produce a rough approximation: the business of philosophy is to make people conscious of the rules of these games. For unless they are conscious of them, they will be unable to play them better, and also unable to see which new games they want to learn to play, and which old games they want to continue to play or to discard. With certain games, the logic of which is fairly simple, philosophy has already succeeded. The rules or principles by which one does science, or mathematics, or formal logic, are now fairly clearly established: and this is partly why these studies have prospered. Other games present more difficulty. How, for instance, does one decide about moral problems, or problems of personal relationships? How is one to assess works of art? How is one to decide whether to have a religion, and which one to have? In all these cases the philosopher's business is neither (as the first view holds) simply to put forward a moral view, a view about personal relationships, a theory of aesthetics or religion, and compare it with other views, leaving the individual to choose for himself—for on what criteria can he choose?—nor (the second view) simply to analyse the language of morals, aesthetics and religion, for this alone does not clarify the rules of the games with sufficient depth. His business is, first and foremost, to make clear how the games are in fact played: to clarify *what it is* to settle a moral issue, *what it is* to have a religion, *what it is* to love or be friends with someone, in the same way as we are now clear about what it is to do science or mathematics.

What kind of process is this clarification? To use the example of science: we might feel that the clarification of the science-game was actually very simple. After all, we are all familiar nowadays with the standard technique of observation with our senses, the formulation of hypotheses, making crucial experiments, framing theories and laws, and making predictions from them. But in fact and in history, it took humanity till the Renaissance to gain a clear idea of this game. The change from a view of the world according to which nature was magical and mysterious to a view which regarded nature as essentially explicable and predictable was long and arduous: men gradually grew out of a belief in magic, and came to have the power to see nature as a collection of *things*, depersonalised objects which could be weighed, measured, analysed and so forth. This sort of change has various aspects to it. Depth psychologists such as O. Mannoni[1] have given a clear account of its psychological nature (the security required to free oneself from the desire to people nature with little men, magical forces, ghosts, spirits, and so on). But it has also an important *conceptual* aspect; and it is this which is the business of philosophy. It is not just a question of how we feel about the world and ourselves: it is a question of *in what terms we conceive them*. This is something which is amenable to rational discussion, in which we may become more conscious of our own concepts, our own language, our own pictures of the world, and hence learn to change them. All of us

[1] *Prospero and Caliban*, by O. Mannoni (Methuen).

are largely unaware of the conceptual principles by which we work: we have, in this century, a reasonably firm grasp of the world of sense-experience, and feel at home with science. But with morals, religion, literature and the arts, and above all in personal relationships we feel lost and bewildered (unless we are already so blind that we think there is nothing to see). Neither of the two views I have criticised earlier cater adequately for this blindness or bewilderment. It is inept to say that we must just try harder or behave better or follow more sensible ways of life: and it is inadequate to say that we must scrutinise our language and become more clever about the logic of words. For our difficulties do not arise either because we are not good or virtuous enough, or because we are not clever enough. They arise because we feel *lost*, out of our depth, groping, trying to learn how to play the various games of life. It is the same sort of feeling that one might have when about to step on to the dance floor without knowing how to dance: one doesn't know how to *start*.

Philosophy, then, is clarification of *method*, of the way in which these games are played. Philosophers are already aware of this in the way they handle certain metaphysical problems, questions like 'Are any of our actions really free?' or 'Can we ever be certain about anything?' We feel about these questions that the most difficult thing is to know how we should *start* setting about giving them an answer. We feel basically puzzled by them: we have no method ready to hand by which we can deal with them. But there are hundreds of questions in life, which are in this sense 'metaphysical': hundreds of questions, that is, which arise because we are trying to play games without being clear about the rules. The classical metaphysical questions—questions about free will, reality, truth, and so on—have always formed only a small intellectual arena in which academicians fight. Meanwhile in the square outside, in the public streets, in the homes and the dance-halls, ordinary people are puzzled by parts of their lives in precisely the same *kind* of way, a way which necessitates education in self-consciousness, in awareness of how they are in fact facing the world and themselves, in overhauling their conceptual equipment. It is this process which I have described as philosophy.

It would require much more careful consideration to investigate the forms which philosophy, in this sense, will take in the future. But it is certainly true that, even if it splits up into various departments designed to clarify and deal with different games, it will still retain more coherence than, say, the physical sciences. For the links between our depth-psychology, our behaviour, our ways of life, our conceptual equipment, our actual beliefs, and the language in which we express them are very binding: and it is doubtful whether any competent philosopher will be able to afford ignorance in any department. For this reason the training of philosophers as linguistic analysts merely is grotesquely inadequate: and one is not surprised at the appearance of counter-symptoms in the shape of thinkers who care nothing for analysis, but who open the door to experiences and life-games that linguistic philosophers prefer to leave standing in the corridor—as for instance the Existentialist school, or the school of German metaphysical theologians. One should also notice groups which plainly ought to connect with philosophy, but which our appalling communications have virtually severed: the two most obvious examples are, first, the psycho-analysts, and second, the Cambridge literary critics.

For these reasons the philosopher should be familiar with, and sympathetic to, all the major fields which relate directly to human concepts: all the studies and forms of creation which can teach, influence, or other-wise affect our conceptual equipment. Obvious candi-dates for study are: literature (particularly the novel and drama), music, psychology, the social sciences and history. All these bear directly—and, for most people, much more effectively than philosophy—on our con-ceptual equipment: on our stance towards life, the spectacles we wear, the game-playing skills we have, the tools we use, the pictures we form. One suspects that academic philosophers have made an obvious error: the error of supposing that only those disciplines which result in true propositions have any bearing upon truth. Thus, it is plain that in the normal sense of 'true', music, painting, drama and even novels do not make 'true' statements: but it is wrong to conclude that they have nothing to do with truth. They may indirectly generate factually true statements by a complex pro-cess, which no one has properly studied, which con-sists roughly in giving us certain experiences and affecting our feelings and emotions in a certain way, and hence disturbing and illuminating us, so that we can then change our pictures of the world and our concepts and eventually make or assent to statements which would previously have cut no ice with us at all. Even though the arts do not assert facts, they still teach us—and teach us rationally. It is this kind of rational teaching that philosophy needs to include within its ambience. In so far as rational discussion takes place in words, the basic and essential part of the philosopher's tool-kit will, of course, be linguistic. But there will be other tools: instead of merely being able to analyse statements, he will learn to relate them to the general world-pictures and the conceptual equipment as a whole of individuals.

This process of philosophy is, of course, itself a game: and a particularly difficult one to play. It is as if philosophy had to move up to a higher storey and watch the people on the ground-floor playing their various games with more or less success, and then assess and criticise their rules; or as if one were presented with a compendium of games in a box, like a Christmas present, only the rules had been left out—one has to try and work out what the games are, how they should be played, and whether they are worth playing at all. All this makes the most stringent demands: a demand for logical rigour, so that the game of philosophy should be purposive and not a mere art-gallery comparison of different concepts, and yet also a demand for breadth of understanding, so that we can keep good communications with all the games that actually exist. Yet the importance of philosophy, at any level of life and in any context, is obvious: for without this process of becoming more aware, more conscious of the rules, it is perhaps impossible to assess or make any deliberate rational change in one's life. Certainly we may change, and live, without philosophy, just as we may without common sense, or without some of the five senses. But we cannot do so effectively. We desperately need a technique to handle the problems involved; and it may be possible, without much further research, for the first time to establish such a technique on a firm footing. For at least we recognise the fields of activity involved— literature, the arts, social science, and so forth—and can begin to think about the methods of each, and the way in which they bear upon the problems of life. We may yet live to see the philosopher really earning his keep.

The analysis of concepts, then, emerges as only one tool in the philosopher's equipment: but a very necessary tool, because it is a very good way of generating consciousness. One thing, at least, everyone can always do: he can always say 'What does that mean?' But if he is content with what we may call a purely *logical* analysis, his increase of consciousness, though helpful, will not be as profound as it might be. For meaning goes deeper than usage: it stems from a man's whole conceptual equipment, which itself is rooted in his personality and past experiences. For this reason we have far more than a purely verbal landscape to map: just as, perhaps, someone who really wished to understand the geography of a country would have to go below the surface of its landscape and understand its geology also—the nature of the subsoil, the history of the rock strata, and so forth. Of course geography is a different subject from geology: and of course, for the sake of simplicity at least, we must count philosophy as a different subject from psychology, history, sociology and so on. But even this is a little misleading. We deceive ourselves if we suppose that these humane studies possess totally separate and discrete subject-matters: it is better to say that there are human problems which can and must be approached both philosophically, psychologically, sociologically and so forth. We need a harmonious team of experts, who are experts in particular methods of approach: not a number of disjoined specialists working in their own studies and laboratories.

Given an approach of this kind, I believe it would be possible to make the methods of philosophy as real and important to the ordinary person as, say, the methods of elementary mathematics, or of reading and writing. The danger, of course, is that the closer union of these varied disciplines may result in none of them being practised with a proper rigour and forcefulness: we may get a kind of optimistic, liberal muddle of vaguely cultural subjects that relate in some way—but not very forcefully or directly—to human problems. This is one of the reasons why I think that the analysis of concepts, which if properly practised is a very exacting discipline, is a good tool to acquire first. But I hope it will also be realised that if we use it in conjunction with other tools, we may achieve results beyond our present expectations.

## CHAPTER IV

# PRACTICE IN ANALYSIS

This is a comparatively short chapter: I have not given a very great number of passages for criticism, nor very many questions of concept to be answered. For this there are several reasons. First, inasmuch as the book is used in sixth forms and for the benefit of any students who face examinations, their teachers will be primarily concerned with the particular kind of general paper relevant to the needs of their particular students: and of course, apart from the fact that they all include questions of concept, these papers vary very widely. Teachers will naturally want to make use of past papers printed by universities and colleges, and direct the attention of their pupils to the sort of passages and questions which these include. Secondly, those who read this book without any examination paper in view are likely to be interested in one field of thought rather than others: thus some will be more concerned with religion, others with politics, others again with morals, and so on. These specific interests are important, because they give an extra incentive for the analysis of concepts: someone seriously concerned with religion is likely to do more justice to the concepts involved in a passage dealing with religion than to those involved in passages dealing with other matters. Thirdly, although this is in some sense a text book, I very much wish to avoid the impression that when the reader has worked through the examples given for practice, he is thereby fully equipped for dealing with all other situations in which analysis is required—that he has, as it were, received a complete inoculation against ambiguity, muddled thinking, or lack of logical awareness. A necessary part of training in analysis consists in being able to recognise passages and questions where analysis is needed, as distinct from merely being able to analyse a given passage or answer a given question. Although no single book can teach this recognition, at least each can try to avoid obscuring its importance.

What the reader should acquire by these practical examples, therefore, is primarily a feeling of confidence: a feeling that he now has a firmer grasp of what *sort* of process the analysis of concepts is. He should certainly not feel—and this would be true however many examples he was made to work through—that he has covered all conceivable cases where analysis is required. Every passage and every question of concept is different from every other. I have tried to pick questions from various fields, and passages from authors of various ages, various interests and various styles, to show something of the diversity of context into which conceptual analysis can enter. But the process of acquiring mastery over analysis is never-ending: and the bulk of the work must, inevitably, be done by the reader himself (with the help of his instructor, if he has one)—when he reads the literature of his chosen interests, listens to the wireless, picks up his morning paper, argues with his friends, or meditates by himself. It is in the striving of the individual, on his own, towards greater logical awareness and understanding that the importance of conceptual analysis as an educational instrument chiefly consists.


## I. PASSAGES FOR CRITICISM[1]

### (1) *Cardinal Newman, 'Apologia Pro Vita Sua'*

Grant that, upon prayer, benefits are vouchsafed, deliverances are effected, unhoped-for results obtained, sicknesses cured, tempests laid, pestilences put to flight, famines remedied, judgments inflicted, and there will be no need of analysing the causes, whether natural or supernatural, to which they are to be referred. They may, or they may not, in this or that case, follow or surpass the laws of nature, and they may do so plainly or doubtfully, but the common sense of mankind will call them miraculous; for by a miracle is popularly meant, whatever be its formal definition, an event which impresses upon the mind the immediate presence of the Moral Governor of the world. He may sometimes act through nature, sometimes beyond or against it; but those who admit the fact of such interferences, will have little difficulty in admitting also their strictly miraculous character, if the circumstances of the case require it. When a Bishop with his flock prays night and day against a heretic, and at length begs of God to take him away, and when he *is* suddenly taken away, almost at the moment of his triumph, and that by a death awfully significant, from its likeness to one recorded in Scripture, is it not

[1] In some of the passages quoted below the authors are not speaking *in propriis personis*, but representing the opinions of characters in their novels or dialogues. This applies to nos. (3), (9), (17) and (20).

trifling to ask whether such an occurrence comes up to the definition of a miracle?

(2) *Barbara Wootton, 'Social Science and Social Pathology' (quoting Eliot Slater: ' The McNaghten Rules and Modern Concepts of Responsibility')*

By his endorsement of the uncompromising doctrine that 'No theory of mental medicine could develop without the working hypothesis of determinism', Slater has effectively dissociated himself from all those whose views we have so far examined. For him the '"free will", on which both law and religion are based, proves a sterile idea. If we attempt to inject it into our analysis of causation it only introduces an element of the unknowable.' Statements about the moral responsibility of other people are, moreover, really only statements about the speaker's own state of mind. When we 'give opinions about the responsibility of others we are really reporting on our own states of mind. Perhaps we are doing little more than identifying ourselves with the criminal and asking ourselves whether or not we could have been guilty of his crime. If we then feel that we could have done it only after going mad, we may give one sort of answer; if we feel that we could have done it, but only by suppressing the whole of our better nature, then we shall give another sort of answer. Responsibility, it is worth noting, does have some meaning subjectively, in our judgements on our own actions. It is only when we apply the concept to the actions of others that it breaks down.'

(3) *G. Lowes Dickinson, 'A Modern Symposium'*

From this it follows that my ideal of a polity is aristocratic. For a class of gentlemen presupposes classes of workers to support it. And these, from the ideal point of view, must be regarded as mere means. I do not say that that is just: I do not say it is what we should choose; but I am sure it is the law of the world in which we live. Through the whole realm of nature every kind exists only to be the means of supporting life in another. Everywhere the higher preys upon the lower; everywhere the Good is parasitic on the Bad. And as in nature, so in human society. Read history with an impartial mind, read it in the white light, and you will see that there has never been a great civilisation that was not based upon iniquity. Those who have eyes to see have always admitted, and always will, that the greatest civilisation of Europe was that of Greece. And of that civilisation not merely an accompaniment but the essential condition was slavery. Take away that and you take away Pericles, Phidias, Sophocles, Plato.

(4) *George W. Hartmann, 'Educational Psychology'*

The combination of sexual maturity and occupational immaturity extending over a decade of vigorous youthful life is all but intentionally designed to violate the most fundamental precepts of mental hygiene. Early marriage is the solution that seems best to conserve all the biological and social values involved, but only a fortunate few appear to be able to arrange for this preferred response. Contraceptive devices are now widely understood and there is little doubt that they have encouraged temporary and experimental unions, the usefulness of which is still uncertain. Deliberate promiscuity on the part of either sex is abnormal, at least in the statistical sense, and usually points to some personality barrier to genuine happiness. Homosexuality is a clinical puzzle in itself, but also a sample of the need for tolerance in appraising many of the inferior modes of sexual adjustment into which individuals fall when their normal emotional development is hampered. Psychologists have no *a priori* right to insist that life-long monogamous marriages are the only happy ones conceivable, but matched against the alternatives commonly attempted, it comes out distinctly in first place. Under these circumstances, it seems but proper that our educational program should be directed toward making this form of family organisation as successful as possible by building attitudes and controls early in life favourable to this outcome.

## (5) *S. Freud, 'The Future of an Illusion'*

One must now mention two attempts to evade the problem, which both convey the impression of frantic effort. One of them, high-handed in its nature, is old; the other is subtle and modern. The first is the *Credo quia absurdum* of the early Father. It would imply that religious doctrines are outside reason's jurisdiction: they stand above reason. Their truth must be inwardly felt; one does not need to comprehend them. But this Credo is only of interest as a voluntary confession; as a decree it has no binding force. Am I to be obliged to believe every absurdity? And if not, why just this one? There is no appeal beyond reason. And if the truth of religious doctrines is dependent on an inner experience which bears witness to that truth, what is one to make of the many people who do not have that rare experience? One may expect all men to use the gift of reason that they possess, but one cannot set up an obligation that shall apply to all on a basis that only exists for quite a few. Of what significance is it for other people that you have won from a state of ecstasy, which has deeply moved you, an imperturbable conviction of the real truth of the doctrines of religion?

### (6) *Walter de la Mare, 'Love'*

On the meaning given to the word love, in all its varieties—love of home, of country, of children, of ideas and ideals—has depended much of the English genius, character and ethical status; and, no less, of the conception of womanhood. The theories of Freudianism have narrowed and adulterated that meaning by concentrating attention on only one of its elements. So too with our dreams. Fantastic or seemingly inane, vivid, intense, illuminating or moving, whatever their relation to our waking life may be, they are a kind of experience. By the imposing of an arbitrary interpretation on them —and no interpretation can be finally refuted—they have been sacrificed not only to sex, for the ramifications of which we are at any rate not responsible, but to a degraded conception of it. So Swift, with his Yahoos, defamed and degraded human nature. Nothing is secure against this privy paw, intent on digging us all up. And certainly not literature and love poems. 'We do not mind being told', says Mr C. S. Lewis in his paper 'Psycho-Analysis and Literary Criticism', 'that when we enjoy Milton's description of Eden some latent sexual interest is, as a matter of fact, and along with a thousand other things, present in our unconscious. Our quarrel is with the man who says "You know why you're *really* enjoying this?" or "Of course you realise what's behind this?"'

(7) *John Locke, 'An Essay concerning Human Understanding'*

If therefore we know there is some real being, and that non-entity cannot produce any real being, it is an evident demonstration that from eternity there has been something: since what was not from eternity had a beginning; and what had a beginning must be produced by something else. Next, it is evident that what had its being and beginning from another must also have all that which is in and belongs to its being from another too. All the powers it has must be owing to and received from the same source. This eternal source, then, of all being must also be the source and original of all power; and so this eternal being must be also the most powerful. Again, a man finds in himself perception and knowledge. We have then got one step further; and we are certain now that there is not only some being, but some knowing, intelligent being in the world. There was a time, then, when there was no knowing being, and when knowledge began to be; or else there has been also a knowing being from eternity. If it be said, there was a time when no being had any knowledge, when that eternal being was void of all understanding: I reply, that then it was impossible there should ever have been any knowledge—it being as impossible that things wholly void of knowledge, and operating blindly, and without any perception, should produce a knowing being, as it is impossible that a triangle should make itself three angles bigger than two right ones.

## (8)  Tolstoy, 'War and Peace'

The presence of the problem of man's freewill, though unexpressed, is felt at every step of history. All seriously thinking historians have involuntarily encountered this question. All the contradictions and obscurities of history, and the false path historical science has followed, are due solely to the lack of a solution of that question. If the will of every man were free, that is, if each man could act as he pleased, all history would be a series of disconnected accidents. If in a thousand years even one man in a million could act freely, that is, as he chose, it is evident that one single free act of that man's in violation of the laws governing human action, would destroy the possibility of the existence of any laws for the whole of humanity. If there be a single law governing the actions of men, freewill cannot exist, for man's will would be subject to that law. The problem is, that regarding man as a subject of observation from whatever point of view—theological, historical, ethical, or philosophic—we find a general law of necessity to which he (like all that exists) is subject. But regarding him from within ourselves, as what we are conscious of, we feel ourselves to be free. This consciousness is a source of self-cognition quite apart from and independent of reason. Through his reason man observes himself, but only through consciousness does he know himself. Apart from consciousness of self, no observation or application of reason is conceivable.

(9) *Charles Williams, 'Shadows of Ecstasy'*

He saw the intellect and logical reason of man no longer as a sedate and necessary thing, but rather a narrow silver bridge passing over an immense depth, around the high guarded entrance of which thronged clouds of angry and malign presences. Often mistaking the causes and often misjudging the effects of all mortal sequences, this capacity of knowing cause and effect presented itself nevertheless to him as the last stability of man. Always approaching truth, it could never, he knew, *be* truth, for nothing can be truth till it has become one with its object, and such union it was not given to the intellect to achieve without losing its own nature. But in its divine and abstract reflection of the world, its passionless mirror of the holy law that governed the world, not in experiments or ecstasies or guesses, the supreme perfection of mortality moved. He saluted it as its child and servant, and dedicated himself again to it, for what remained to him of life, praying it to turn the light of its awful integrity upon him, and to preserve him from self-deception and greediness and infidelity and fear. 'If $A$ is the same as $B$' he said, 'and $B$ is the same as $C$, then $A$ is the same as $C$. Other things may be true; for all I know, they may be different at the same time; but this at least is true.'

(10) *Dorothy Sayers, 'Unpopular Opinions'*

Or take again the case of the word 'reality'. No word occasions so much ill-directed argument. We are now emerging from a period when people were inclined to use it as though nothing was real unless it could be measured; and some old-fashioned materialists still use it so. But if you go back behind the dictionary meanings—such as 'that which has objective existence' —and behind its philosophic history to the derivation of the word, you find that 'reality' means 'the thing thought'. Reality is a concept; and a real object is that which corresponds to the concept. In ordinary conversation we still use the word in this way. When we say 'those pearls are not real', we do not mean that they cannot be measured; we mean that the measurement of their make-up does not correspond to the concept 'pearl', that, regarded as pearls they are nothing more than an appearance; they are quite actual, but they are not real. *As pearls*, in fact, they have no objective existence. Professor Eddington is much troubled by the words 'reality' and 'existence'; in his 'Philosophy of Physical Science' he can find no use or meaning for the word 'existence'—unless, he admits, it is taken to mean 'that which is present in the thought of God'. That, he thinks, is not the meaning usually given to it. But it is, in fact, the precise meaning, and the only meaning, given to it by the theologian.

## (11) *Matthew Arnold, 'The Function of Criticism'*

Force and right are the governors of this world; force till right is ready. *Force till right is ready*; and till right is ready, force, the existing order of things, is justified, is the legitimate ruler. But right is something moral, and implies inward recognition, free assent of the will; we are not ready for right,—*right*, so far as we are concerned, *is not ready*,—until we have attained this sense of seeing it and willing it. The way in which for us it may change and transform force, the existing order of things, and become, in its turn, the legitimate ruler of the world, will depend on the way in which, when our time comes, we see it and will it. Therefore for other people enamoured of their own newly discerned right, to attempt to impose it upon us as ours, and violently to substitute their right for our force, is an act of tyranny, and to be resisted. It sets at nought the second great half of our maxim, force till right is ready. This was the grand error of the French Revolution; and its movement of ideas, by quitting the intellectual sphere, ran, indeed, a prodigious and memorable course, but produced no such intellectual fruit as the movement of ideas of the Renaissance.

(12) *Dorothea Krook, 'Three Traditions of Moral Thought'*

The empiricist believes that the observed facts of men's moral behaviour will yield not only descriptive but also prescriptive generalisations or 'principles'; and this is the belief that determines (and, for him, justifies) his method of enquiry. But the belief is wholly delusory. The vital transition, from what is to what ought to be, can never be effected by the method of merely cataloguing and classifying and analysing the observed behaviour of men. For knowledge of what is will never yield a knowledge of what ought to be so long as 'what is' refers only to the actual and takes no account of the possible. It can only do so when the notion of 'what is' is referred to some view of human possibility, as distinct from mere human actuality. For men 'ought to be' what they are 'ideally' capable of being: this is the only proper meaning of the word 'ought' in this context; and this necessarily implies some ideal of man, some view of human possibility as distinct from actuality. The empiricist, accordingly, who prides himself on being free from any preconceptions about human possibility, who claims to be unimpeded in his enquiries into morals by any ideal of human possibility, any view of what men might be as distinct from what men are, is, on this analysis, fatally deluded.

## (13) *Susan Stebbing, 'Thinking to Some Purpose'*

Dr Ernest Barker raises the question: 'But is Communism, in any real sense of the word, a faith?' He replies: 'Faith demands some affirmation of belief in things apprehended but invisible: it is a venture of spiritual courage, which leaves the pedestrian ground and takes to the wings of flight. The whole philosophy of Communism is resolutely opposed to faith. It is a philosophy of material causation; and its devotees are vowed to the study of material causes and the production of material effects.' To this Mr Hamilton Fyfe replied: 'Dr Ernest Barker limits unduly the meaning of "faith" when he says "the whole philosophy of Communism is opposed to faith", and defines "faith" as "belief in the invisible". Communists have faith in human nature, faith that Right will triumph over Might (though they do not leave Right unarmed), faith in the emergence of justice and comradeship from the welter of struggling and selfish cut-throat competitors, faith that equality of chances in life will give better results than the harsh and undeserved social distinctions of our present system.' First, Dr Barker distinguishes between 'a real sense of the word' and, presumably, some unreal sense. This distinction is surely meaningless, or else a flagrant begging of the question in favour of some 'sense of the word' that suits one's own argument. Secondly, Mr Fyfe, in calling attention to Dr Barker's definition of 'faith', protests that its meaning is unduly limited if it be defined as 'belief in the invisible', but he at once goes on to maintain that the Communists have faith in what I, at least, should have supposed to be also 'the invisible'.

(14)  *T. S. Eliot, 'Religion and Literature'*

It is simply not true that works of fiction, prose or verse, that is to say works depicting the actions, thoughts and words and passions of imaginary human beings, *directly* extend our knowledge of life. Direct knowledge of life is knowledge directly in relation to ourselves, it is our knowledge of *how* people behave in general, in so far as that part of life in which we ourselves have participated gives us material for generalisation. Knowledge of life obtained through fiction is only possible by another stage of self-consciousness. That is to say, it can only be a knowledge of other people's knowledge of life, not of life itself. So far as we are taken up with the happenings in any novel in the same way in which we are taken up with what happens under our eyes, we are acquiring at least as much falsehood as truth. But when we are developed enough to say 'This is the view of life of a person who was a good observer within his limits, Dickens, or Thackeray, or George Eliot, or Balzac; but he looked at it in a different way from me, because he was a different man; he even selected rather different things to look at, or the same things in a different order of importance, because he was a different man; so what I am looking at is the world as seen by a particular mind'—then we are in a position to gain something from reading fiction. We are learning *something* about life from these authors direct, just as we learn something from the reading of history direct; but these authors are only really helping us when we can see, and allow for, their differences from ourselves.

## (15) *Bernard Shaw, Preface to 'St Joan'*

Criminal lunatic asylums are occupied largely by murderers who have obeyed voices. Thus a woman may hear voices telling her that she must cut her husband's throat and strangle her child as they lie asleep; and she may feel obliged to do what she is told. By a medico-legal superstition it is held in our courts that criminals whose temptations present themselves under these illusions are not responsible for their actions, and must be treated as insane. But the seers of visions and the hearers of revelations are not always criminals. The inspirations and intuitions and unconsciously reasoned conclusions of genius sometimes assume similar illusions. Socrates, Luther, Swedenborg, Blake saw visions and heard voices just as St Francis and St Joan did. If Newton's imagination had been of the same vividly dramatic kind he might have seen the ghost of Pythagoras walk into the orchard and explain why the apples were falling. Such an illusion would have invalidated neither the theory of gravitation nor Newton's general sanity. What is more, the visionary method of making the discovery would not be a whit more miraculous than the normal method. The test of sanity is not the normality of the method but the reasonableness of the discovery.

(16) *Simone Weil, 'The Need for Roots'*

The notion of obligations comes before that of rights, which is subordinate and relative to the former. A right is not effectual by itself, but only in relation to the obligation to which it corresponds, the effective exercise of a right springing not from the individual who possesses it, but from other men who consider themselves as being under a certain obligation towards him. Recognition of an obligation makes it effectual. An obligation which goes unrecognised by anybody loses none of the full force of its existence. A right which goes unrecognised by anybody is not worth very much. It makes nonsense to say that men have, on the one hand, rights, and on the other hand, obligations. Such words only express differences in point of view. The actual relationship between them is as between object and subject. A man, considered in isolation, only has duties, amongst which are certain duties towards himself. Other men, seen from his point of view, only have rights. He, in his turn, has rights, when seen from the point of view of other men, who recognise that they have obligations towards him. A man left alone in the universe would have no rights whatever, but he would have obligations.

(17) *Plato, 'The Apology'*

We should reflect that there is much reason to hope for a good result on other grounds as well. Death is one of two things. Either it is annihilation, and the dead have no consciousness of anything; or, as we are told, it is really a change—a migration of the soul from this place to another. Now if there is no consciousness but only a dreamless sleep, death must be a marvellous gain. I suppose that if anyone were told to pick out the night on which he slept so soundly as not even to dream, and then to compare it with all the other nights and days of his life, and then were told to say, after due consideration, how many better and happier days and nights than this he had spent in the course of his life— well, I think that the Great King himself, let alone any private person, would find these days and nights easy to count in comparison with the rest. If death is like this, then, I call it gain; because the whole of time, if you look at it in this way, can be regarded as no more than one single night. If on the other hand death is a removal from here to some other place, and if what we are told is true, that all the dead are there, what greater blessing could there be than this, gentlemen?

(18) *Aristotle, 'The Art of Poetry'*

Tragedy is essentially an imitation not of persons but of action and life, of happiness and misery. All human happiness or misery takes the form of action; the end aimed at is a certain kind of activity, not a quality. Character gives us qualities, but it is in our actions— what we do—that we are happy or the reverse. In a play accordingly they do not act in order to portray the Characters; they include the Characters for the sake of the action. So that it is the action in it, i.e. its Fable or Plot, that is the end and purpose of the tragedy; and the end is everywhere the chief thing. Besides this, a tragedy is impossible without action, but there may be one without Character. We maintain, therefore, that the first essential, the life and soul, so to speak, of tragedy is the Plot; and that the Characters come second—compare the parallel in painting, where the most beautiful colours laid on without order will not give one the same pleasure as a simple black-and-white sketch of a portrait.

(19) *St Augustine, 'Confessions'*

When therefore I did will anything, or not will it, I was most certain that it was I and no other that willed or did not will it; and I did even observe that the cause and root of my sin lay there. But whatsoever I did unwillingly, I saw that I did suffer rather than do, and I esteemed that not to be a fault but a punishment; and I quickly confessed—when I remembered that Thou art just—that I was not punished unjustly. But yet again I said: 'Who made me? Is it not God, Who is not only Good, but is even Goodness itself? Whence then come I thus to will that which is evil, and not to will that which is good, by means whereof I may come thus to be justly punished? Who placed this power in me, and who engrafted upon my stock this branch of bitterness, seeing that I was wholly made by my God, most sweet? If the devil be the author thereof, whence is that same devil? And if he himself, by his own perverse will, from a good angel became a devil, whence grew that will to be wicked in him, seeing that he had been made all good angel by that most good Creator?' By these cogitations I was again depressed.

### (20) *Lawrence Durrell, 'Clea'*

Something more, fully as engrossing: I also saw that lover and loved, observer and observed, throw down a field about each other ('Perception is shaped like an embrace—the poison enters with the embrace', as Pursewarden writes). They then infer the properties of their love, judging it from this narrow field with its huge margins of unknown ('the refraction'), and proceed to refer it to a generalised conception of something constant in its qualities and universal in its operation. How valuable a lesson this was, both to art and to life! I had only been attesting, in all I had written, to the power of an image which I had created involuntarily by the *mere act of seeing* Justine. There was no question of true or false. Nymph? Goddess? Vampire? Yes, she was all of these, and none of them. She was, like every woman, everything that the mind of a man (let us define 'man' as a poet perpetually conspiring against himself)—that the mind of man wished to imagine. She was there forever, and she had never existed!

### (21) *A. J. Ayer, 'The Problem of Knowledge'*

The answers which we have found for the questions we have so far been discussing have not yet put us in a position to give a complete account of what it is to know that something is the case. The first requirement is that what is known should be true, but this is not sufficient;

not even if we add to it the further condition that one must be completely sure of what one knows. For it is possible to be completely sure of something which is in fact true, but yet not to know it. The circumstances may be such that one is not entitled to be sure. For instance, a superstitious person who had inadvertently walked under a ladder might be convinced as a result that he was about to suffer some misfortune; and he might in fact be right. But it would not be correct to say that he knew that this was going to be so. He arrived at his belief by a process of reasoning which would not be generally reliable; so, although his prediction came true, it was not a case of knowledge. Again, if someone were fully persuaded of a mathematical proposition by a proof which could be shown to be invalid, he would not, without further evidence, be said to know the proposition, even though it was true.

## (22) *Cyril Connolly, 'Enemies of Promise'*

In point of fact there is no such thing as writing without style. Style is not a manner of writing, it is a relationship; the relation in art between form and content. Every writer has a certain capacity for thinking and feeling and this capacity is never quite the same as any other's. It is a capacity which can be appreciated and for its measurement there exist certain terms. We talk of a writer's integrity, of his parts or his powers, meaning the mental force at his disposal. But in drawing from these resources the writer is guided by another consideration; that of his subject. One might say that the style of a writer is conditioned by his conception of the reader, and that it varies according to whether he is writing for himself, or for his friends, his teachers or his God, for an educated upper class, a wanting-to-be-educated lower class or a hostile jury. Style then is the relation between what a writer wants to say; his subject—and himself—or the powers which he has: between the form of his subject and the content of his parts. Style is manifest in language. The vocabulary of a writer is his currency but it is a paper currency and its value depends on the reserves of mind and heart which back it. The perfect use of language is that in which every word carries the meaning that it is intended to, no less and no more.

## (23) *Erich Fromm, 'Man for Himself'*

The contemporary human crisis has led to a retreat from the hopes and ideas of the Enlightenment under the auspices of which our political and economic progress had begun. The very idea of progress is called a childish illusion, and 'realism', a new word for the utter lack of faith in man, is preached instead. The growing doubt of human autonomy and reason has created a state of moral confusion where man is left without the guidance of either revelation or reason. The result is the acceptance of a relativistic position which proposes that value-judgements and ethical norms are exclusively matters of taste or arbitrary preference and that no objectively valid statement can be made in this realm. But since man cannot live without values and norms, this relativism makes him an easy prey for irrational value systems. He reverts to a position which the Greek Enlightenment, Christianity, the Renaissance and the eighteenth-century Enlightenment had already overcome. The demands of the State, the enthusiasm for magic qualities of powerful leaders, powerful machines and material success become the sources for his norms and value-judgements.

## (24) *K. R. Popper, 'The Poverty of Historicism'*

In strong opposition to methodological naturalism in the field of sociology, historicism claims that some of the characteristic methods of physics cannot be applied to the social sciences, owing to the profound differences between sociology and physics. Physical laws, or the 'laws of nature', it tells us, are valid anywhere and always; for the physical world is ruled by a system of physical uniformities invariable throughout space and time. Sociological laws, however, or the laws of social life, differ in different places and periods. Although historicism admits that there are plenty of typical social conditions whose regular recurrence can be observed, it denies that the regularities detectable in social life have the character of the immutable regularities of the physical world. For they depend upon history, and upon differences in culture. They depend on a particular *historical situation.* Thus one should not, for example, speak without further qualification of the laws of economics, but only of the economic laws of the feudal period, or of the early industrial period, and so on; always mentioning the historical period in which the laws in question are assumed to have prevailed.

(25) *C. P. Snow, 'The Two Cultures and The Scientific Revolution'*

A good many times I have been present at gatherings of people who, by the standards of the traditional culture, are thought highly educated and who have with considerable gusto been expressing their incredulity at the illiteracy of scientists. Once or twice I have been provoked and have asked the company how many of them could describe the Second Law of Thermodynamics. The response was cold: it was also negative. Yet I was asking something which is about the scientific equivalent of 'Have you read a work of Shakespeare's?' I now believe that if I had asked an even simpler question—such as, What do you mean by mass, or acceleration, which is the scientific equivalent of saying 'Can you read?'—not more than one in ten of the highly educated would have felt that I was speaking the same language. So the great edifice of modern physics goes up, and the majority of the cleverest people in the western world have about as much insight into it as their neolithic ancestors would have had.

(26) *Arthur Koestler, 'Neither Lotus nor Robot'*

And why must the Master and his pupils write book after book to explain that Zen cannot be explained, that it is 'literally beyond thought, beyond the reach of thought, beyond the limits of the finest and most subtle thinking', in a word, that it cannot be put into words? We know that not only mystical experience defies verbalisation; there is a whole range of intuitions, visual impressions, bodily sensations, which also refuse to be converted into verbal currency. Painters paint, dancers dance, musicians make music, instead of explaining that they are practising no-thought in their no-minds. Inarticulateness is not a monopoly of Zen: but it is the only school which made a philosophy out of it, whose exponents burst into verbal diarrhoea to prove constipation.

(27) *Hans Meyerhoff, 'Plato among Friends and Enemies'*

We may reject the particular kind of fiction invoked by Plato, or the purpose it serves in the *Republic*. But before we vent our moral indignation on Plato or use this passage as the sole basis for the extreme charge that he advocated 'lying propaganda', we might also pause to reflect that Plato (as usual) was dealing with a fundamental problem of social theory. After Marx, Nietzsche, Sorel and Freud it would be naïve to deny that fictions, or myths, have played and continue to play a crucial role in politics. Thus it is disingenuous, to say the least, to twist Plato's recognition of this fact into the charge that he advocated 'lying propaganda'—all the more so, if the critic's own political vocabulary cannot dispense with myths in disguise. For, according to Mr Popper, the ultimate moral values which we choose as goals for the good society are 'decisions' or 'conventions', which are not rationally justifiable and which invariably contain 'a certain element of arbitrariness'. Now, if liberty and equality are chosen as ultimate moral values, not on rational grounds, but by an ineluctably arbitrary act of will, or faith, do they not have the logical status of political myths?

(28)  *W. H. Auden, 'The Fallen City'*

At his best, the worldly man is one who dedicates his life to some public end, politics, science, industry, art, etc. The end is outside himself, but the choice of end is determined by the particular talents with which nature has endowed him, and the proof that he has chosen rightly is worldly success. To dedicate one's life to an end for which one is not endowed is madness, the madness of Don Quixote. Strictly speaking, he does not desire fame for himself, but to achieve something which merits fame. Because his end is worldly, that is, in the public domain—to marry the girl of one's choice, or to become a good parent, are private, not worldly, ends— the personal life and its satisfactions are, for the worldly man, of secondary importance, and should they ever conflict with his vocation, must be sacrificed. The wordly man at his best knows that other persons exist, and desires that they should—a statesman has no wish to establish justice among tables and chairs—but if it is necessary to the achievement of his end to treat certain persons as if they were things, then, callously or regretfully, he will.

(29) *Sir Arthur Eddington, 'The Philosophy of Physical Science'*

Let us suppose that an ichthyologist is exploring the life of the ocean. He casts a net into the water and brings up a fishy assortment. Surveying his catch he proceeds in the usual manner of a scientist to systematize what it reveals. He arrives at two generalisations:

(1) No sea-creature is less than 2 inches long.

(2) All sea-creatures have gills.

These are both true of his catch, and he assumes tentatively that they will remain true however often he repeats it. In applying this analogy, the catch stands for the body of knowledge which constitutes physical science, and the net for the sensory and intellectual equipment which we use in obtaining it. The casting of the net corresponds to observation: for knowledge which has not been or could not be obtained by observation is not admitted into physical science. An onlooker may object that the first generalisation is wrong. 'There are plenty of sea-creatures under 2 inches long, only your net is not adapted to catch them.' The ichthyologist dismisses the objection contemptuously. 'Anything uncatchable by my net is *ipso facto* outside the scope of ichthyological knowledge, and is not part of the kingdom of fishes which has been defined as the theme of ichthyological knowledge. In short, what my net can't catch isn't fish.'

## (30) *Geoffrey Gorer, ' The Marquis de Sade'*

As a man, Sade is important as a paradigm. Except in his honesty and his easy access to his deepest unconscious wishes, there is no reason to think him unique. Despite the efforts of the psychoanalysts, we still know very little of the reasons which make artistic creation so imperative for some people. With its reductionary, historical approach to human development, psychoanalysis tends to see artistic creation as a successful sublimation of repressed sexual or para-sexual infantile wishes, and would probably explain Sade's failure as a dramatist by the fact that his repressions were not strong enough, that he 'acted out' too much. But another interpretation seems to me possible: it seems possible that this mysterious drive for creativity is very primitive in some individuals; and that, when this drive is thwarted either by technical incapacity or public indifference, there is a 'back-formation' to more direct sado-masochism, rather than the reverse, that the sado-masochism is a substitute for creativity, rather than the creativity a sublimation of infantile drives. Had Mussolini been a successful dramatist or Hitler a successful architect, the history of this century might have been very different.

### QUESTIONS TO ANSWER

(1) To what extent is education a political issue?

(2) Is there such a thing as international law in the world today?

(3) Is the distinction between classical and romantic a useful tool for literary criticism?

(4) 'The prime purpose of the artist is to represent his own feelings on canvas.' Discuss.

(5) What is the subject-matter of mathematics?

(6) Could there ever be a science of human nature?

(7) In what sense, if·any, can we properly speak of poetic truth?

(8) Does the coherence of every state depend on a common morality?

(9) 'If God does not exist, everything is permitted.' Discuss.

(10) Is Communism a religion?

(11) Are there any other kinds of explanation besides scientific explanation?

(12) Could one ever construct a robot in all respects like a man?

(13) Do animals think?

(14) Was England a democracy before the introduction of votes for women?

(15) Are there any absolute values? How could they be established?

(16) Will the historian ever be able to make accurate predictions?

(17) 'All men are born equal.' Discuss.

(18) Is it ever meritorious to do actions which we enjoy doing?

(19) 'I think: therefore I exist.' Is this a good argument?

(20) Is it ever right to do something immoral?

(21) What is a totalitarian state?

(22) 'Beauty is in the eye of the beholder.' Discuss.

(23) Do all novels have a moral purpose?

(24) If my actions were all predictable, would they ever be free?

(25) In what sense, if any, does music ever tell us anything?

(26) 'Property is theft.' Discuss.

(27) Could the existence of God ever be proved?

(28) 'The Chancellor was responsible for the economic collapse.' 'Metal fatigue was responsible for the aircraft crashing.' Is 'responsible' used in the same sense in both these sentences?

(29) In what respects do laws of nature differ from the moral law?

(30) 'There is no such thing as naturalistic drama.' Discuss.

(31) What is the difference between education and indoctrination?

(32) 'Germany is a less adult nation than Great Britain.' What could be meant by this?

(33) Is any literature to be censored on grounds of obscenity alone?

(34) How far does imagination come into the work of the historian?

(35) On what general grounds, if any, should the state curtail the liberty of the individual?

(36) Can we ever be quite sure that what we see is not illusory?

(37) 'Nothing is more certain than the truths of geometry.' Discuss.

(38) What logical difficulties impede translation from one language into another?

(39) How far would the concept of morality apply to a man on a desert island?

(40) Is it possible to distinguish between form and content in poetry?

(41) Do electrons exist in the same sense that tables exist?

(42) 'Cadbury's means good chocolate.' What does 'means' mean here?

(43) How far does the progress of science depend on intuition?

(44) 'Latin trains the mind.' What evidence would count for or against this statement?

(45) Is a scientific theory ever conclusively verifiable?

(46) Would you place the first chapter of Genesis under the heading 'fact' or 'fiction'?

(47) Is it possible to distinguish accurately between an invention and a discovery?

(48) 'Virtue is its own reward.' Discuss.

(49) 'We can never become aware of the unconscious mind, since it is by definition unconscious.' Is this true?

(50) Is there such a thing as 'learning to think', without reference to any particular field of study?